AKC

brilliant

manager

brilliant

manager

third edition

What the best managers know, do and say

Nic Peeling

Prentice Hall
is an imprint of

Harlow, England • London • New York • Boston • San Francisco • Toronto • Sydney • Singapore • Hong Kong
Tokyo • Seoul • Taipei • New Delhi • Cape Town • Madrid • Mexico City • Amsterdam • Munich • Paris • Milan

PEARSON EDUCATION LIMITED

Edinburgh Gate
Harlow CM20 2JE
Tel: +44 (0)1279 623623
Fax: +44 (0)1279 431059
Website: www.pearsoned.co.uk

First edition published in 2005
Third edition published in Great Britain in 2010

Pearson Education is not responsible for the content of third party Internet sites.

Portions of this text are adapted from *Dr Peeling's Principles of Management:
Practical Advice for the Front-Line Manager* (ISBN: 978-0-932-63354-5),
Copyright © 2003 by Nic Peeling, with permission from Dorset House
Publishing (www.dorsethouse.com).

ISBN 978-0-273-74323-1

British Library Cataloguing-in-Publication Data
A catalogue record for this book is available from the British Library

Library of Congress Cataloging-in-Publication Data
Peeling, Nic.
  Brilliant manager : what the best managers know, do and say / Nic Peeling.
-- 3rd ed.
    p. cm.
  Includes bibliographical references and index.
  ISBN 978-0-273-74323-1 (pbk. : alk. paper) 1. Management--Handbooks,
manuals, etc.
I. Title.
  HD38.15.P44 2010
  658--dc22

                                                              2010034353

10 9 8 7 6 5 4 3 2 1
15 14 13 12 11 10

Cartoon illustrations by Bill Piggins
Typeset in Plantin by 3
Printed and bound in Great Britain by Henry Ling Ltd, Dorchester, Dorset

To Sue, Harriet, Jilly, Julie and Sally

Contents

About the author

Nic Peeling had 15 years' experience as a front-line manager at QinetiQ – a leading international defence and security company. Nic is now semi-retired and works as a Trusted Expert for QinetiQ and is a Visiting Fellow at the Defence College of Management and Technology at Cranfield University. Formerly an award-winning software researcher, he has a doctorate from the Computing Laboratory at Oxford University.

Nic remembers vividly all the mistakes he made in the process of becoming an experienced manager – experiences that have driven his interest in discovering and distilling what brilliant managers and leaders know, do and say.

Visit **www.nicpeeling.com**

Introduction

Welcome to the third edition of *Brilliant Manager*. A quarter of the second edition was new material, and again for this third edition a quarter of the book is new. The second edition contained a replacement chapter called *Brilliant business tips*; a new chapter called *Management master-class*; and a substantial rewrite of the chapter on *Organising your team*. For this third edition all the material on leadership is new. Chapter 2, called *Leadership*, has been totally rewritten. I now believe that too much is made of leadership styles and that most brilliant leaders use the same core techniques. The leadership chapter now describes these techniques, which if applied will make you a great leader. One of the attributes of a brilliant leader is to have a credible vision, strategy and plans for the future of the team and its offerings. The new Chapter 3, *Visions, strategies and plans*, describes how to create such visions, strategies and plans.

Although this new edition contains a lot of new material, the basic principles of management I described in the first edition remain unchanged. I believe there is a very clear distinction between good and bad management. The fact that we all laugh at Dilbert means that we all have the same idea about what bad management is. Perhaps more surprisingly, anybody lucky enough to work for a brilliant manager will probably find that all the rest of the team have an equally good opinion of their boss. Generally, it's easy to see good and bad management in other people. However, it's far less easy to see it in yourself, and harder still to know what it is that you need to change to become a brilliant manager.

What is it that brilliant managers know, do and say that makes them so good at their jobs? If you want to know . . . read on. The good news is that most brilliant managers use a very similar set of core techniques – this book will show you what they are, and how to adopt them for yourself.

Brilliant Manager is for anyone who is a frontline manager, dealing directly with staff, customers, senior management and the like. This book distils the hard-won experience of the best managers and sets it down as practical things you need to know, do and say.

The sections covered are:

Managing people – Very few managers receive training in managing difficult staff issues. Making the wrong decision could cause someone real pain. This thought should scare you. How do you make sure you handle every situation the right way?

Leadership – You are not just a manager: your team is looking to you for direction, inspiration, and to confront tough problems – and you thought managing people was scary! What techniques do brilliant leaders use?

Visions, strategies and plans – A great leader knows where the team and its offerings are going. How do you create brilliant visions, strategies and plans?

Culture – Some teams have great team spirit and obviously share the same values and aspirations. How do you foster a strong team culture?

Managing different types of people – Different professions (lawyers, IT staff, sales people, consultants) all bring their own problems, as do creative staff and support staff. How do you best manage these different types of people?

Organising your team – As a team grows in size, the pressures on you will build up. How do you manage these pressures using tried and tested techniques?

Brilliant business tips – Even if you do not have specific financial responsibility for profit and loss, your job is to focus on defining and delivering your team's products and services, and to market them to your customers. What are the top tips you need to follow to make you a good business manager?

Managing your organisation – The better your team delivers results, the more others in your organisation will see it as a threat. There will be a constant stream of initiatives from your own organisation that seem to be designed to stop your team doing its job. You have to act as the interface between your team and the rest of the organisation. Losing your temper is not the way to handle this role – but what is?

Management master-class – What are the answers to the typical questions that would be asked in a management master-class?

Knowing it, doing it, saying it – There is a massive gulf between the theory and practice of management. A number of real-life examples will help bridge that gulf.

Literal reading warning

I am assuming you are a busy person. I want you to read this book, so I have kept it short and written in a style that is easy to read. However, there are dangers in the style that I use:

- You may take me too literally. I exaggerate and simplify some points to help them hit home. My aim is to help you think about the issues, not to produce a recipe that can be followed precisely. Every management job has its own unique context, and this book must be interpreted sensibly in the context you work within. For example, if your team is losing lots of money you will need to adopt a management approach that is appropriate to what is probably a life or death situation – ER doctors do not usually have the time to discuss treatment with their patients!

● I will make issues seem simpler than they really are. You may read parts of this book, think you understand the points being made, and then not know what to do in a real-life situation. I think that the theory of management is simple – it's the practice that's hard and it cannot be learned from a book. What I have tried to do is to provide a framework for you to think about your job and to make lots of suggestions for techniques that you might like to try.

The golden rule of management

Before moving on to the rest of the book I want to start with the single most important rule of management:

You will be judged by your actions, not by your words, and your actions set the example for your team to follow.

The implications of this rule will appear time and again, in numerous different forms, throughout this book.

Your actions set the example for your team to follow

Acknowledgements

I would like to thank my employers QinetiQ for allowing me the use of work facilities to write the first and second editions of this book.

I am indebted to Neil Hepworth, who read each chapter as it was first written and gave me such encouragement and sound advice during the creation of this book.

I was most fortunate in having so many friends and colleagues who read the book and gave me feedback on it, including Mark Gamble, Cath Hipwood, Ken and Christine Magowan, Steve Mitchell, Michael O'Mahony, Eric Peeling, Thomas Petford, Jutta Spaniol, Sally and David Rees, Rob Rowlingson, Julian Satchell, Mike Wild, Arthur Williams and Harriet Yeoman. I am particularly indebted to Richard Chisnall, Duncan Machray, Betty Mackman, Matthew Peck, Anne-Marie Rocca and Alan Watson for their line-by-line critiques of early drafts.

I had many hundreds of conversations and interviews with friends, associates and colleagues about the subject matter of the book, and it is impossible to name them all individually; you know who you are and please accept my thanks.

I am very greatful to John Clark for his help creating the third edition.

Finally, thanks to the team at Pearson Education and, in particular, to my publisher Rachael Stock for believing so strongly in my book. Thanks also to Samantha Jackson, my publisher for the second edition, and to Martina O'Sullivan for the third edition.

CHAPTER 1

Managing people

The thought of writing this chapter was what motivated me to write this book in the first place. Let's face it, the average standard of managing people is far from brilliant, so this is a very good place to start a book about becoming a brilliant manager.

I would like to start with an optimistic observation:

People in a work context are very forgiving. If your performance improves then your staff will very soon forget your past lapses.

This means that you can turn round the team's view of your management style very quickly indeed.

I will also restate the golden rule of management in an appropriate form:

The simplest way to get your staff to behave in a particular way is to behave that way yourself.

Fundamental principles of managing people

One of the problems that managers face when managing people is that they often have not accepted the fact that the principles of people management are very similar to the principles of being a good parent or a good teacher, namely:

- setting high expectations of people's performance and behaviour that is appropriate to their abilities;

- setting clear boundaries of acceptable behaviour;
- imposing discipline and, where necessary, punishment when behaviour is unacceptable;
- setting clear boundaries of acceptable performance; working with underperforming staff to improve their performance; if performance cannot be improved in your team you must decide if individuals need to leave your team or, in extremis, whether they need to leave the organisation;
- providing clear, immediate feedback on performance and behaviour; praise good performance, and constructively criticise poor performance;
- personally setting an example of the performance and behaviour you expect;
- behaving in a way that wins the respect of your team.

Being a parent or teacher is a great responsibility. Brilliant managers have to accept that they are doing a job with similar levels of responsibility. You may find this uncomfortable as a manager, but your staff will have no trouble at all accepting that this is the way brilliant managers should behave.

Is management manipulation?

I would really like to believe that you can be a manager without being manipulative, but there will be times when a manager has got to be manipulative. The uncomfortable truth is that when resolving all the different pressures from existing customers, your own organisation, bids for new business and the like, you are inevitably going to have to persuade people to do things that are not entirely in their own interests. It is also an uncomfortable truth that you are not always going to be in a position where you can explain the bigger picture to all your staff. All that you can hope to achieve is that your manipulation is moral. My definition of moral manipulation would be:

If your team knew the whole picture, the majority would support your actions.

One of the reasons for mentioning the issue of manipulation is that many managers complain that their staff are suspicious of their motives. It basically comes down to whether your staff respect and trust you. Staff suspicion is quite natural and you can only create the necessary levels of trust and respect by your openness, honesty and integrity. Trust and respect are essential if your decisions are going to be widely accepted. This raises a key issue:

How open should you be?

A good starting point is to be as open and honest *as possible*. The problems lie in defining what that nasty get-out clause 'as possible' means in practice. I will tackle this issue by listing the circumstances in which I believe less than total openness is acceptable:

- *When you have to respect confidentiality.* You may be instructed by your organisation to keep certain information confidential, or you may not be able to release information that was told to you in confidence.

- *When you have to support 'the corporate line'.* This will be discussed in more detail in a later chapter.

- *When full openness would cause unnecessary pain.* For example, you may be discussing how a member of your team can improve their performance. You may need to be selective about telling the staff member about their failings in order that they can handle – and respond positively to – your criticism.

- *When full disclosure will unnecessarily depress your team.* A good example might be the latest initiatives from head office. Many of these never actually get implemented in a way that is as threatening as they first appear. My approach to such issues is to openly answer any questions about them. I always try to go occasionally to group gatherings, e.g. at coffee time, so that people can quiz me. In this way I make it clear that there is no secret about what is going on, but I also imply that I am relaxed about such things, and that when, or if, they impinge on the team I will immediately brief everyone.

● *When the effort of communication is not worthwhile.* You will never have enough time to communicate with your team as much as you would like. This means you have to prioritise your communication, and consequently some issues will drop off the bottom. The next section discusses this further.

How to organise communications in your team

I will start with two slightly depressing observations. First, no matter how well you manage the communications within your team, it is likely that most of your team members will feel they are not kept properly informed. Second, under the pressures most managers face, the first thing to suffer is usually communications.

I wish I could lay out an easy plan for you to follow, but the best I can do is lay down a few useful guidelines.

*Ensure that matters that **directly** affect staff are discussed with them before irrevocable decisions are taken*
It is a well-known psychological effect that people who feel that they have no control over their environment become anxious, stressed and demotivated. Consequently, the maximum irritation comes from staff finding out that decisions that affect them directly have been taken without any consultation with them.

you do not have to do all communication personally

I suggest you make such matters your top communication priority. Remember that you do not have to do all communication personally; you can use other members of your team's organisation as appropriate.

brilliant tip

It is good practice to make sure that you give bad news personally. Try to give people bad news before they find it out from the rumour mill. Give bad news face-to-face and not via email or memo.

Make yourself available for informal questions

If your team see that you are not hiding away from their questions, they are much less likely to think you are deliberately keeping things from them.

Keep formal communication meetings short, regular and separate from other routine meetings

Formal communication meetings are truly awful for all concerned – both you and your team will probably despise them. However, such meetings have some invaluable features. You will put them in your diary so they will tend to happen regularly. They show that you are regularly available for complaints to be made directly to you, and as a result can release pressures that are building up in the team. A common mistake is to allow the agony to drag on and on. I suggest a rigid time limit of less than an hour be adhered to.

Use email to chat to team members

Email is a really efficient mechanism for short, chatty updates. It's also a good method of quickly communicating messages to several people at once.

Remember that communication should be a two-way process

When you make yourself available so that your team can ask you questions, you can ask them questions as well. In addition, you will probably have regular one-to-one meetings with your staff, which you can use to probe their views. If you are one of those lucky people who are naturally good listeners then this will be easy; if you are like the rest of us, keep practising those listening skills.

Handling difficult staff issues

Some staff require much more management effort than others. I single out three different types of staff who require particularly careful handling. First, there are staff who are underperforming; then there are your key staff who you really do not want to lose; and lastly there are staff who take up a lot of your time but who are not really valuable to your business.

Handling underperforming staff

The first point to make is:

You must tell your staff if they are underperforming.

This may sound obvious, but you might be surprised how many managers do not face up to this task. There are, however, good ways to do this as well as bad ways.

Distinguish between misconduct and other forms of underperformance

This section is about helping underperformers to improve their performance. However, it is possible that the problem is one of misconduct rather than underperformance. Laziness, poor timekeeping and the like represent misconduct and the person should be told firmly to mend their ways.

When disciplining, or firing, someone, do it 'by the book'.

Much of this section describes how to help someone get over their problems, but you must always be aware of the fact that the situation could get to a stage where you need to instigate formal proceedings against one of your underperforming staff. Different countries have different laws governing unfair dismissal. Different organisations have different processes for handling misconduct and underperforming staff. Find out exactly what your company processes are and follow them to the letter. If you have a good personnel department, they will probably be able to offer you support and advice. There are times to do things by the book, and this is one of them!

> different countries have different laws governing unfair dismissal

Identify the cause of the problem

There are two key issues to determine: first, is the staff member guilty of misconduct, or is it a case of underperformance? If it is misconduct then they need to be told firmly to behave. Otherwise, you need to ensure that you both understand the problem, decide how you can help, and then tell them how you expect them to address the problem.

brilliant tip

Never tolerate misconduct. Misconduct should be treated with zero tolerance. Deal with misconduct as soon as possible after it comes to light. Make sure of your facts before confronting someone with an accusation.

When supplying constructive criticism you must not blame the person

The purpose of explaining a person's failings to them is to help them address the problems caused by those failings. If you blame them for their failings they are very unlikely to listen to any constructive criticism.

Set achievable, measurable targets for improvement

It is important that underperforming staff know precisely what is expected of them. Targets must be sensibly challenging and the achievement of them easy to measure.

Do not bear a grudge

After disciplining a staff member or giving constructive criticism, both you and the person concerned may feel uncomfortable in dealing with each other. You must set the tone by dealing with them as if nothing had happened. If the person sulks then you need to decide whether it's best to ignore it, or whether they would respond to you having a quiet word with them to reinforce the fact that you are trying to help them to recognise a problem and to learn from it.

A person's failings are often the flip side of a strength

For example, someone with great personal drive may be impatient of others with less drive. In such circumstances you should acknowledge the positive attribute and suggest that the negative aspects are recognised and managed by the individual, even though they are unlikely to ever totally overcome their failings.

Never undermine a person's self-respect

Respect is key to a healthy team – both respect for self and respect for each other. Just because someone is not thriving in their current job in your team does not mean that they would not blossom if given a different job; or moved to a different team; or moved out of your organisation.

Have a consistent view of how patient you will be with underperformers, and beyond that act ruthlessly

Staff need to know that they have a reasonable amount of time to address problems. They also need to know you will properly analyse the reasons for underperformance and address those causes, even if it means a move of job, or a change of manager, or some other remedy. However, your team cannot carry passengers indefinitely – they are a potential threat to the survival of the team. In addition, it is not kind to leave a person struggling – almost everyone wants to do a good job, so the person involved is probably unhappy. Once you have decided that the person has been given sufficient time to improve, you need to decide, with appropriate consultation with your superiors and/or personnel department, whether the person is redeployed or fired. If the person is to be fired then follow the procedures outlined in the following pages.

Make sure you use any probationary period to weed out underperformers

It is astonishing how many underperformers were spotted during a probationary period but managed to make it through on to the permanent staff. In many countries and many organisations it is vastly easier to fail a probationer than fire an underperformer.

> it is vastly easier to fail a probationer than fire an underperformer

Many managers worry how the team will react to firm management action against underperformers. Provided you allow a reasonable time for improvement, you may well be surprised that most team members would be more ruthless than you are – after all, they have to carry the passengers.

Termination

Imagine that the worst possible scenario has occurred and one of your team has to be terminated. How do you do it?

The first thing to say is that unless you are instructed otherwise you should do it yourself and not leave it to your personnel department, or anyone else, to do – you should 'shoot your own dog'.

The second thing you should do is check that you have done everything properly *and have the necessary documentation to prove it*. Have all the processes been followed through? If not, work out with personnel how you can best implement any processes that were missed.

You will need to talk to personnel anyway, to find out what your organisation's processes are for termination. You should also be alert to the very rare cases where you are concerned about the person having an extreme reaction to being terminated. If you are concerned that the person may become irrational, distraught, violent or want to seek revenge, then you should work with the personnel department to manage these risks.

The third thing to do is to decide what will happen after the termination. Will the person be taken to clear their desk and then escorted off site? Or can you trust the person to do all this without an escort? Or will the person be working out a period of notice? Do you need to get their keys and any other company property off them? Do you need to disable their access to computer systems? Are you sure they will be safe to drive or do you need to arrange a taxi, or for someone to drive them home?

Before describing the three key steps to a termination interview it is worth making a few general points.

You must remain calm and businesslike

If you have done things properly, the person being terminated should not be surprised. This does not mean that the person will not be very shocked – they probably will be. The kindest thing you can do is to be calm and businesslike, as this will help them to maintain control and keep their dignity.

Keep the termination interview as short as possible

The meeting will be agony for the person being dismissed, they will probably be in shock, and hence prolonging the interview is cruel.

Avoid getting sucked into discussions or negotiations

By this stage the die is cast, and you need to make it clear that an irrevocable decision has been made, and that the termination interview is pretty much one-way communication – from you to them. You will probably feel empathy for the person being fired, but you must avoid expressions of sympathy that open up the chance for prolonged discussions.

Be totally honest
Any lack of honesty on your part is both unfair and can get your organisation into serious legal trouble.

The termination interview

The form of a termination interview comprises three clear steps.

1 Inform the person that an irrevocable decision has been made to terminate them.

2 Tell the person clearly and truthfully why they are being terminated. Give the background, so as to make it clear that all the organisation's processes have been followed to the letter.

3 Describe the mechanics of termination. What will happen after the interview: how they will collect their personal belongings; when they must leave; whether there is a severance package; whether you can give them a reference; what paperwork needs completing; how any pay outstanding will reach them, etc.

Post-termination actions

You need to decide how you are going to tell the team about the termination, and also any customers the person had inter-actions with. You need to perform a difficult balancing act that combines honesty with an approach that does not blacken the person's reputation. You must remember that you cannot be sure that the person who was terminated will not contact other team members and customers. For example, you need to ensure that customers are comfortable that they will continue to enjoy as good a service from your team now that the person has left your organisation.

I sincerely hope you will need the advice in this section on termination very infrequently.

Handling your key staff

Why should you handle your key staff any differently from the rest of your team? Your innate feelings of fairness will probably lead you in the direction of 'equal treatment for all'. An additional benefit of equality of treatment is that you will defuse internal tensions caused by accusations of favouritism. However, there are differences that you should acknowledge.

- Key staff will often have superstar qualities and, as mentioned earlier, there is often a negative flip side to great qualities. It is only reasonable that you are willing to invest management time in helping with the negative aspects of genius. In my own world of research scientists there is a common saying that the line between genius and insanity is often blurred – this is a total lie . . . *line, what line?!*

- Key staff will usually know their value to you, and will often be tempted to use that power to their advantage. Anyone else trying this trick is very easy to deal with!

brilliant tip

Do not pretend that you are not dependent on your key staff. I have seen managers try to downplay the value of their most important people – do managers really think their top people are that stupid? It is certainly true that no one is indispensable, and that in extremis the team will survive, but do not try to minimise the value of your key staff.

Keep a dialogue going with your key staff

Most staff leave their jobs as the result of some small issue that becomes the straw that breaks the camel's back. Keeping close contact with your key staff will not only spot the 'straws', but will also allow you to keep the 'backs' from getting near to breaking point. Staff will usually drop hints about grievances, so you need to be on the lookout for problems. Sorting out such problems is much easier

> staff will usually drop hints about grievances

and cheaper if they are handled before the situation reaches crisis point. It is obviously important that you recognise who your key people are. Remember they are not just the flashy superstars; do not overlook the quieter types who are key to keeping your business alive.

A good team culture is the best protection

If your key staff value the respect of the other team members, they will not want to lose that respect by being overly demanding. A gentle 'I am worried how that will look to the rest of the team' can sometimes work wonders.

Do not yield to threats

You have to decide how far you are going to go to keep your key staff, and then be consistent in sticking to your line. Most organisations will not pay a salary that matches what a poacher will offer. In my view you cannot respond to a threat to leave by matching the poaching salary – it will cause such dissent among your other key staff that the situation will quickly get out of hand. Your best hope is to find that some other issue started the person looking outside in the first place, and that by addressing that initial grievance you can turn them around.

Do 'succession planning'

It is a significant risk to be very dependent on any member of your team. Part of your job is to do succession planning for key staff members. You will not always have the luxury of being able to have someone ready to take over immediately a key person leaves, but it is worth working out in advance how you will cope.

When you lose a key member of the team, do it with good grace

It is surprising how often your paths are likely to cross again. They may even want to have their old job back. There is almost no situation in which you benefit from someone leaving your team on bad terms with you.

Handling low-value/high-maintenance staff

Your key staff will often require significant investment of your time, but in most cases you will invest this time willingly because of their value to your business. There will be other staff who also require a lot of your time, but who are of only marginal value to your business. There are staff who will constantly moan about the way you and your organisation treat them. There are staff who think they are much better than they really are, and who will never understand why their talents are not appreciated. There are people whose personalities cause them to fan the discontent of others. You can probably add plenty of other types of personality to this list! How do you deal with such staff?

The most obvious solution to this problem is to avoid it in the first place. Try to spot such staff during your recruitment processes and do not hire them. If you spot one of these staff during a probationary period, and cannot cure their problem, then fail the probation.

No matter how hard you try, you will get problem staff who are not key to your business. The first thing to do is to work out if their problem can be solved, even partially, by making them aware of the problem. If so, then this is the place to start. There will, however, be staff whose fundamental personality traits mean they will be a constant problem. An example of this sort of person is the staff member who thinks they are much better than they really are.

What do you do about the high-maintenance, low-value staff? I recommend you calculate whether they are worth the management effort. If not, then you can either be ruthless about rationing the amount of time you spend on them, and/or you can look for every opportunity to move them out of your team. For example, you can tell someone who thinks they are better than they really are that you do not have as high an opinion of them as they have of themselves, and that maybe they need to find a different environment

> if they are the bad apples I urge you to be brutal

in which they can reach their full potential. If you find these ideas too brutal then you can carry your problem staff and hope they eventually leave. This is fine, provided that their problems only affect *you*; if they are the bad apples in your team barrel then I urge you to be brutal.

It is very important that you do not give in to this sort of person in order to keep them quiet. You must not give them higher pay rises than they deserve, and you must not give in to unreasonable demands. If you do, you deserve the discontent you will get from the rest of your team.

Staff development

Although I have serious doubts about the value of formal career development plans, I am convinced of the need to do regular appraisals of staff performance. Your organisation may mandate annual appraisals, but even if it does not, you should review the performance of staff at least once a year. I tend to perform such appraisals in the run-up to salary reviews. There are a number of different aspects that can be included in such an appraisal but I think there is one issue that dominates all others.

Are there some aspects of a person's performance or behaviours that you feel they should improve?

If there is some way that an individual can improve their worth to the organisation, they are entitled to be told about it. It sounds obvious, but time and again I see managers failing in this duty.

A typical structure for a staff appraisal would be:

- Review the person's performance during the assessment period. Highlight what you felt they did well and also those areas where they failed to meet your expectations. Check whether they agree with your assessment, and discuss any differences. Ultimately it is your view that counts, but they should have the opportunity to challenge your assessment.

- Give a thumbnail sketch of what you consider to be the person's strengths and weaknesses. Cover both their professional capabilities and also their behaviours. When discussing behaviours separate their behaviours within the organisation from their behaviours with customers. Identify any areas where you would like them to address weaknesses in the next assessment period, which would increase their value to the team and your organisation.

- Discuss their aspirations for the future. Find out what challenges would particularly excite them. Consider any changes to their current role that you or they think would be beneficial.

- You may decide to discuss their career aspirations as regards pay and promotion. If you do this, remember to be realistic. It is unacceptable to give people a too rosy view of their future.

- Fill in any necessary paperwork required by your organisation, such as the review of past objectives and the setting of new objectives.

Given that I do not believe that brilliant managers rely on formal career development processes, the next section describes the key technique that brilliant managers use.

The right job, for the right person, at the right time

Allocating staff to the right jobs should be one of a manager's highest priorities. Regrettably the commonest form of allocating staff can be summed up as:

'I have a job that needs doing; Natasha is free; she can do it.'

Or, putting it another way:

'I have a square hole; I have a round peg; pass me a hammer.'

The problem with doing it properly is that you make yourself a lot more work:

'I have a square hole; the square pegs are already in use; use one of the square pegs which fits particularly well; one of my

I have a square hole; I have a round peg; pass me a hammer

triangular pegs could grow to fit that newly available square hole; but that triangular peg is currently in use; . . .'

Growing a staff member's capabilities is largely achieved by finding the right job to stretch them at the appropriate time. To do this you must understand what are the particular strengths of each member of your team, and choose jobs for them that utilise and grow those strengths. I am often surprised, and dismayed, how often people are deployed on jobs that do not play to their strengths. Indeed, it often seems to be a policy to give people jobs that play to their weaknesses, in the mistaken belief that this will help them strengthen one of their weak areas.

brilliant tip

You need to act in a confident manner . . . without coming across as overly confident or arrogant. The correct level of confidence will help establish your authority.

brilliant dos and don'ts

Don't take the credit but do accept the blame

There is a very simple rule to follow:

The team gets all the credit, you get all the blame

If the team screws up, you can criticise your own staff, but do not allow any of your superiors to do so – they can shout at you, not your team.

Don't assume an open door is enough

It has become traditional for managers to tell their team that 'my door is always open'. I suggest that a much more powerful message to tell your team is:

*You **must** tell me when you are unhappy or have a grievance.*

This will help create an environment in which your staff do not bottle up their unhappiness or anger.

Do apologise when you make a mistake

When was the last time your boss apologised to you? An apology, genuinely offered, will usually be accepted. Knowing that you can apologise when you make mistakes can be a great stress reducer for you. Go on, give it a try! This is a special case of the more general rule that follows.

Do be polite

Can anyone tell me why so many managers seem to ignore the demands of common courtesy? What your mother taught you about saying *please* and *thank you* applies equally to the workplace as it does to your social and family lives. Remember to praise staff who have done a job well. The golden rule of management also tells you that by being courteous yourself, courtesy will become an integral part of the team culture.

Do keep your promises to your staff

On the surface this sounds obvious, but the issues become clearer if it is reworded as *do not make promises you cannot keep*. Remember how busy you are and avoid the temptation to offer things that you are not sure you will have the time to deliver on. Most broken promises are not deliberate; nor are they broken because you could not deliver; they are broken because you were too busy to deliver. The best solution is not to have made the promise in the first place.

Another reason that promises get broken is that the situation can change in a way that makes it impossible to keep your promise. In this situation you need to explain why it is no longer possible to honour your promise.

Don't trust the wrong people

I know this is not a very helpful comment to make – how do you know who to trust? There are basically two ways to find out who to trust: first, you can be a good judge of character and, second, you can see who is respected by the team. The second method only requires sufficient contact with the team and competent observational skills, and I recommend it to you. One of the most common mistakes I have seen new managers fall into is to develop a close and trusting relationship with someone the team does not respect.

Don't give your staff unpleasant surprises

If you have to do something that a staff member is not going to like, try to ensure it does not come 'out of the blue'. For example, make sure you have discussed with staff what the outcome of a pay review is likely to be before they receive formal notification of their pay increase. Another example is that if you are going to have to formally warn a member of the team about underperformance, make sure they know well in advance that there are concerns about their performance. Staff can easily, and justifiably, feel aggrieved if unpleasant things happen to them without any warning.

Don't be inconsistent

Behaviour that can be interpreted as inconsistent will greatly undermine your authority with your team. In a number of places in this book I am advocating that you take hard, and at times ruthless, action. It is important that you maintain a reputation of 'hard but fair'. The two ways to do this are: first, apply the golden rule of management and be as hard, or harder, on yourself as you are on others; second, ensure that you are consistent, and hence even-handed, in your treatment of your staff.

Don't set unrealistic deadlines

I am even opposed to so-called *stretch* deadlines. Such research as there is in my field of expertise (computer software) tends to back up my own observation that very tight deadlines demotivate, and unrealistic deadlines totally demotivate. Research even shows that self-imposed tight deadlines often lead to demotivation. This observation may seem to be counter-intuitive, but I suggest you try some experiments.

Do set the team's targets and incentives very carefully

Targets and incentives do motivate particular forms of behaviour, and well-chosen targets and incentives can work extremely well. However, do not be surprised if your team responds to any targets and incentives you set, to the single-minded exclusion of everything else. Some managers seem to love setting lots of targets and offering numerous incentives as a means of motivating staff; I just wish they would realise that targets and incentives are a very crude mechanism that often lead to behaviour patterns that are not in the team's interest.

Don't pretend you know more than you do

Some managers hate admitting they do not know something. The team will respect you much more if you freely admit your ignorance and ask to be informed. Asking stupid questions is a sign that you are not stupid.

Don't tolerate office politics within the team

Office politics, and the ambitious, small-minded people who play such games, can quickly undermine a good team spirit. I suggest you stamp hard on the first signs of politics infecting your team. A good sign of staff playing politics is when they do not behave in an obvious, straightforward way; if you cannot see what the motivation is for someone's actions, it can be worth checking what they are up to.

Do empower people to do things differently from you, and to possibly fail

Empowerment is a much-abused word. You must think carefully beforehand whether you are delegating a task that you can afford to have done badly. You need a clear view of how you are going to check the progress being made on the delegated task and the extent to which the person doing the task is being overseen. Too often a task is delegated and then at a later date the manager panics and puts in a detailed review process. It is a sad fact that most people only learn through their own mistakes, so you have to eventually let people have the full responsibility for a task – just make sure it is a task the failure of which you can recover from.

A second aspect of real empowerment is that you have to school yourself not to interfere if someone does a task very differently from the way you would have done it. If you see problems with the way they are doing a job then you may wish to alert them to the possible dangers, but if they are responsible then they must make the final choice of how to do the job.

Do give trust before it has been earned

This is a corollary of the last point. Your staff will not grow until they
have made the mistakes that all inexperienced staff have to make for
themselves. You have to be tolerant of these mistakes, provided that people
are not making the same mistake over and over again. The upshot of this
is that you have to give trust to staff who have not yet earned that trust,
because if you do not they will never grow to become trustworthy
people.

Don't go to meetings that will undermine your staff

This is yet another corollary of empowerment. As the boss you will often
be invited to meetings relating to tasks you have delegated others in
your team to lead on. You must remember that your presence will often
significantly change the nature of a meeting, and people will naturally look
to you for leadership. Consequently, your presence can easily undermine the
empowerment you have given to team members.

Do be aware that you may need to overreact

It is all too easy to underestimate how hard and fast you need to react
to staff problems. It is fairly obvious that issues such as harassment,
discrimination and health and safety will need strong and rapid responses.
It is less obvious that problems such as underperformance, staff morale
and retention can deteriorate very rapidly indeed. Provided you do not
overreact to everything, thereby giving the impression of panic, overreaction
seldom does harm, but underreaction can have very serious
consequences.

Do know when to leave a problem alone

I have just flagged the need to be alert to the possibility that you will
have to react hard and fast to certain problems. Surprisingly, the opposite
technique, which I call benign neglect, can also be very useful. In certain
circumstances, for example when people are getting overly emotional, it
can be useful to move very slowly. Managers are often *action-orientated*
personalities and it can be quite hard to just leave a problem alone
and let nature take its course. Unfortunately there is no magic test to

distinguish those problems that need a rapid response from those that will benefit from benign neglect – it is something you can only learn through experience.

Do remember to have fun

Managing your staff is much easier if you can inject some informality and humour into your interpersonal relationships with your team. You may need to consciously make yourself relax a bit and let your team know it's OK to have fun. As a member of a race of compulsive anal-retentives I know what I am talking about.

So many work environments are high-pressured these days, and so many managers are overworking and stressed out, it is all too easy to take all the fun out of work. Remember there is more to your working life than your pay cheque, and loosen up a bit.

It's OK to have fun

Speaking of the fact there is more to life than work . . .

Do draw a line between work and home

There is no right place to draw the line between your work and your home life. If I see a tendency it is for people to allow the demands of work to cut deeper and deeper into the time you should be devoting to your family and social activities. I suggest you 'draw a line in the sand' between work and home, and try to stick to it.

It is very possible you will draw your line between work and home in a place that some in your team will find uncomfortable. Because of the golden rule of management, your team will by default take your line as the line you want everyone to adopt. I suggest you make it very clear that everyone has to draw their own line and that, within reason, you will respect their decisions and not undermine those decisions by constantly pressuring them to work anti-social hours. One of the less desirable features of a strong culture is that it can coerce people to do things they are not comfortable with; a long-hours culture is one of the commonest examples of this effect that I have seen.

Do beware of sex

There is a well-recognised link between sex and power, so there is a real danger of there being a sexual undertone between yourself and team members of the opposite sex. Hence the following puritan rules:

No flirting of any sort with team members of the opposite sex.

No sexual comments or jokes of any kind.

No casual touching.

If disciplining a staff member of the opposite sex, make sure you have a witness present (e.g. from personnel).

Beware of late one-to-one meetings with staff members of the opposite sex.

And definitely no sexual relationships with team members.

Should you be foolish enough to ignore this last rule then tell your boss about the relationship immediately.

This advice is written from the viewpoint of countries where there is a serious risk of complaints of sexual harassment. Readers need to interpret my advice in the light of the prevailing conditions – what is acceptable in Italy is different from what is acceptable in the UK, which is different from the situation in the USA. I would, however, point out that in all countries the situation seems to be moving in a direction where managers need to be very careful.

Do take a no-tolerance approach to harassment and discrimination

Many countries now have stringent anti-harassment and anti-discrimination legislation covering issues such as gender, race, age and disability. In some countries employees suing for harassment or discrimination has become a growth industry. You must play any harassment or discrimination allegations, against yourself, against a member of your team, or made by a member of your team, *by the book*. Know your organisation's procedures, notify your boss and the personnel department immediately, and be scrupulous in following procedures.

You need to give a strong lead, and also to protect yourself, so:

Almost all comments or jokes about sensitive issues such as gender and race are unacceptable.

Disapprove immediately you hear any such comments or jokes from team members.

Remember to check your processes, e.g. recruitment, for possible complaints of discrimination.

Summary

This chapter, more than any other, is a collection of the techniques that will help make you a brilliant manager. Most of them, I think you will instinctively know, make sense. The less obvious aspects of this chapter are:

- Managing staff involves facing difficult issues, particularly the problems of underperforming staff. The only way to handle these problems is in a tough but fair manner. Be polite; treat people with respect; but expect high standards.

- It is worth investing time in managing your key staff properly.

- Getting the allocation of the right people to the right jobs is key to developing staff.

- Make sure you give bad news personally.

- Make yourself accessible, both formally and informally, for questions from your team.

- Remember – **the team gets all the credit, you get all the blame.**

CHAPTER 2

Leadership

You cannot be a manager without also being a leader. Every chapter in this book covers both management and leadership issues but in this chapter we will focus specifically on the leadership dimension of your job. It is likely that leadership is what scares you most, and from my own observations it is the key area that distinguishes the brilliant manager from less effective managers.

Brilliant managers make tough decisions; they don't run away from difficult problems; they use their power and authority to tackle those problems; and they accept that they are responsible for ensuring that their team survives and thrives … to name but a few of a leader's jobs! This would be a pretty daunting prospect were it not for the fact that most brilliant leaders use exactly the same techniques to be effective leaders. This chapter describes those techniques and by using them you can become a very effective leader.

Create a vision and strategy

There is an old joke that an Army officer had an annual report which included the following comment:

His men follow him … if only out of a sense of curiosity.

A key part of being a leader is to create a vision of the future that your staff will follow you towards.

Creating a credible, achievable vision of the future is not an easy undertaking. It must encompass your overall business strategy and plans, as well as the strategy and plans for your individual offerings. Chapter 3 will provide you with a structured approach to creating visions, strategies and plans.

brilliant tip

A very large part of your time will be taken up with urgent fire-fighting of the problems that will emerge on an almost daily basis. Most managers are aware of the difference between an urgent job and an important job. Creating a compelling vision, strategy and plans is one of your most important jobs. It is essential to ensure that the urgent fire-fighting does not stop you taking the time needed to create your team's vision of the future.

It is reputed that when Napoleon was considering promoting an officer he would often ask, 'Is he lucky?' My belief is that most people have a similar number of potentially lucky breaks. The lucky person is the one who spots when they have encountered a potentially lucky opportunity and pursue it. A good strategy will help you to identify when an opportunity coincides with your vision of the future, and hence that it should be pursued.

It is no good having a great vision of the future, if you then fail to communicate that vision to your team, your superiors and other relevant parts of your organisation. This will almost certainly mean that it has to be written down. It is also less likely that your team will buy into the strategy if you didn't consult them when creating it. You have to personally lead the creation of visions and strategies, but you must ensure that everyone in the team has the chance to make their contribution.

> you have to personally lead the creation of visions and strategies

> **brilliant** tip
>
> Many visions, strategies and plans are created and then neglected. They must be living documents. Chapter 3 will address the ways in which these documents can be both complete and concise.

You will have failed as a leader if your team don't have sufficient respect and trust in you to follow you towards your vision. One of the main objectives of *Brilliant Manager* is to help you behave in a way that will generate that respect and trust.

Set a good example

The golden rule of management is also the golden rule of leadership – your actions will set the example for your team to follow. Chapter 4, *Culture*, will examine this issue in depth.

The golden rule also states that you will be judged by your actions, not by your words. It is worth adding that leaders are judged much more by their actions than their appearance or charisma. This is not to say that you shouldn't dress the part – you should; and even if you are not a charismatic personality everyone can make the effort to show confidence and commitment while still retaining a polite approach.

Face problems

In the previous chapter, *Managing people*, I stressed that a brilliant manager must confront underperformers and those guilty of misconduct. A brilliant leader must take this further so that all major problems are dealt with. One of the reasons that most good leaders are thought to be tough is that they are people who do not sweep problems under the carpet. Another reason that good leaders are thought to be tough is that they don't always search for the easy compromise but meet problems head on and act to fully resolve difficulties.

brilliant tip

When the team as a whole faces a problem, then it is a leader's job to make the team aware of that problem. One of the benefits of having a team strategy is that this strategy can be used to tell the team how problems are being tackled.

And the next tip …

brilliant tip

Problems need to be faced sooner rather than later. Hard and fast action and constant monitoring is often the only way to stop a problem getting worse.

Listen

Without exception, all the great leaders I have encountered make great efforts to talk regularly, one to one, with their team members. There are many benefits to being a good listener.

- Most brilliant leaders are not democrats and accept full responsibility for their decisions. Listening ensures that the team will feel that you make well-informed decisions.
- Nothing does more for morale than knowing your leader listens to you.
- You will find out about problems at an early stage.
- You will get direct access to important intelligence, about

customers, market trends, other staff members, rumours ...
in short, everything!

- You will get lots of advice that you can use to develop a
better strategy and make better decisions.
- It will help you understand your team members, which will
help you to manage them more effectively.

brilliant tip

A common mistake is to talk to your staff soon after taking over
as leader, but to then allow the pressures of daily life to force such
one-to-one sessions out of your agenda. You need to constantly
remind yourself that this is one of your most important duties.

If there is one single thing that you take away from this chapter,
then it should be to talk to your team regularly on a one-to-one
basis.

brilliant example

As an example of how to have the right idea and then ruin the
implementation consider the busy boss who went round the office to talk
to people when he finished work at about 7pm. Unsurprisingly he was
accused of favouring the workaholics.

brilliant tip

You need to find out whose views in the team are widely respected.
You do not want to be seen placing too much weight on the advice
of people whose opinions are not well regarded. Be warned ... this
is a common problem.

Communicate

Not only are brilliant leaders good listeners but they also tend to be excellent communicators. Elsewhere in this book I cover actions such as:

- disseminate your strategy and plans;
- hold regular team meetings;
- take part in conversations at coffee, lunch and round the water cooler;
- send chatty email updates.

brilliant tip

Avoid management speak. If you find your team are playing buzzword bingo with your communications then stop it!

Be customer-focused

A leader has to show that they understand the real priorities. Much of your time will be spent ensuring the team runs smoothly and efficiently. However, the brilliant leader always remembers that their organisation pays for the team to deliver value to external and/or internal customers. You must take a personal interest in delivering that value. In addition to listening to your staff, you need to listen just as intently to your customers. In addition to solving problems within your team you need to give the highest priority to solving customers' problems and for them to see that you put their interests foremost.

> you need to give the highest priority to solving customers' problems

Be cost conscious

I stressed above that you should focus on the outputs of your team. You also need to set high expectations that you will deliver quality outputs for the least amount of money. I recommend that you focus on 'value for money' rather than just driving all costs down to the minimum.

Maintain energy, momentum and agility

A busy leader can easily become the bottleneck that prevents rapid progress and fast changes of direction. There is little worse than working for a boss who doesn't keep on top of their email inbox, who cannot make rapid decisions to solve urgent problems or pursue important new opportunities, and who doesn't follow up on actions they say they'll do later. Chapter 6, *Organising your team*, will give you many techniques that will help you maintain energy, momentum and agility within your team.

> **brilliant** tip
>
> A useful trick is to frequently do a fast pass through your latest emails so that you can spot urgent issues, whilst dealing with your other emails more leisurly.

Some key techniques are:

- delegate appropriate tasks and roles;
- if possible have a good deputy;
- design processes for your team that are as lightweight as possible, and have sufficient visibility to correct any problems that occur;
- be willing to reverse decisions that are shown to be wrong, and if necessary explain why the initial decision was wrong.

Develop your leadership style

It sounds obvious that everyone is different, so everyone's leadership style will be different, but this is overly simplistic. Over the years I have come to realise that all brilliant leaders tend to have very similar components on which they build their style. Like good chefs, the seasoning of the dish will vary, and they will tweak the ingredients, but the basics of the recipe will usually be similar. So what is the recipe?

You cannot be 'one of the gang'

People talk about the loneliness of leadership, and there is sadly a lot of truth in this cliché. A leader has to be somewhat detached from the rest of the team. The leader has the power to affect people's lives, and good leaders are not afraid to use their power to address problems and to ensure the long-term success of the team.

> ### brilliant tip
>
> Don't try to be liked. Don't confuse being respected with being liked. It is essential that a leader be respected, but it is irrelevant if you are liked. Courting popularity is an excellent recipe for not being respected.

Be tough, but fair and respectful, and not a bully

I have already described why most brilliant leaders are seen to be tough. Toughness is an attribute that can be seen as either positive or negative. When combined with fairness and respectful behaviour then toughness will usually be seen in a positive light. If toughness degenerates into bullying then it will probably be viewed negatively.

brilliant tip

You need to avoid subtle forms of bullying. For example, talking over people, refusing to give people priorities when they are overworked, not offering help when someone isn't coping, losing your temper frequently, offering unconstructive criticism, etc. It is essential that you distinguish between sensitive staff and those with thick skins, and talk to them appropriately.

Being tough without bullying is an art.

brilliant tip

The best leader I have personally encountered went beyond tough and was widely viewed as extremely ruthless. Because of his positive qualities, and because the situation he was addressing was seen as very serious, he was widely respected.

Be enthusiastic, passionate and optimistic

If you are blessed/cursed with a charismatic personality then it is likely that you naturally have an enthusiastic, passionate and optimistic nature. Less charismatic personalities have to work at projecting enthusiasm, passion and optimism. There is a lot of evidence that we can all develop our behaviours in a more positive direction. Some of the techniques used can be described as 'monkey do, monkey feel'. The simplest example is that if you make yourself smile and stand up straight you will start

> if you stop voicing negativity you will start to feel more positive

to feel happier. If you stop voicing negativity you will start to feel more positive. If your team hear you talk about things that can be done to make life better, you will feel, and be perceived to feel, more optimistic. Other techniques can be used to train your mind to think about positive and negative events in an optimistic manner. There are many books available to help you develop a more optimistic outlook.

Have a clear set of values

I was originally going to talk about integrity rather than values. Indeed many brilliant leaders rely on their innate integrity to guide all their actions. I widened the word from 'integrity' to 'values' because some good leaders can compromise their integrity and still retain the respect of their team. One example I have seen is where a leader will sometimes say that 'the end justifies the means' and will be willing to inflict significant damage if the benefit to the team is large enough. Another example is when leaders are aggressively competitive for new business. In such cases the team must be clear where the boundaries lie, so they can predict what will be seen as acceptable behaviour. In other places in this book I point out that management is not always black or white – this is such a case, where reality can be worryingly grey.

brilliant example

I knew a very good leader who was aggressively competitive. He did however make it clear that he would not tolerate any illegal behaviour, or any actions that might lead to his organisation being sued.

Be consistent

One of the benefits of having a clear set of values is that your behaviour will be consistent and predictable. A little bit of unpredictability spices life up, but more than a little will undermine the team's trust in you.

Be open

I am using a very broad definition of open, which includes:

- be willing to discuss as wide a range of issues as possible;
- be open to criticism;
- be open to new ideas, new opportunities and new ways of doing things;
- give straight answers to straight questions … don't act like a politician;
- have a truly open door policy.

Openness is one of the best ways a management style can generate trust.

---

brilliant example

You need to avoid behaving in ways that destroy openness. For example when somebody brings you bad news, don't shoot the messenger. Another example is to stop saying 'don't bring me problems, bring me solutions' because people will stop bringing you problems.

Be visible

Brilliant leaders are always highly visible and available to their team. There is a lot to be said for the technique attributed to Hewlett Packard … 'Management by Walking About'.

brilliant example

I knew a manager who although he sat in an open plan office seemed to be welded to his computer, always fiddling with spreadsheets. When approached by a member of his team he would only stop long enough to arrange a time to talk later.

Have the right attitude to detail

Brilliant leaders are never micro-managers, but they always seem to be happy, or even delighted, when they need to dive down into the detail of a problem. A leader has to be seen to be unafraid to handle important details. Sometimes the devil is truly in the detail.

> sometimes the devil is truly in the detail

Even if the detail relates to an area in which you are not an expert, insist that it is explained to you in terms you can understand.

Trust and empower your staff, but ...

Your staff will be comfortable that the flipside of empowerment is that you will hold them accountable for their actions. You will also need to maintain sufficient visibility that problems can be spotted and solved quickly. Even though you hold your staff accountable, you must personally accept the responsibility when dealing with your superiors.

Control your ego

- Exercise your power appropriately, without becoming overly status conscious.
- Don't use delegation as an excuse to use your team members as your servants.
- Be careful about offering and accepting lavish entertainment.

- Remember to say please and thank you.
- Don't assume everyone has to organise their diaries to suit you.

Summary

At first reading this chapter might seem a bit daunting. Sadly, my observation would be that the average standard of leadership is pretty low. As a consequence, if you apply even a few of the techniques described in this chapter you will probably be regarded as a good leader. My selection of the most important aspects of leadership would be:

- be tough, but fair and respectful, and not a bully;
- be enthusiastic, passionate and optimistic;
- be visible;
- listen to your team members – on a one-to-one basis;
- have a credible strategy for the future ... read the next chapter carefully!

Suggested reading

Collins, James C. and Jerry I. Porras (2004) *Built to Last: Successful Habits of Visionary Companies.* New York, Harperbusiness.

A very well-researched book that examines what distinguishes the very best companies from other good companies. The book identifies leadership as a key differentiator, and although the subject matter is about large organisations many of the lessons about leadership apply to small teams as well.

CHAPTER 3

Visions, strategies and plans

I n Chapter 2 I said that a brilliant leader should create a credible vision of the future. This vision should encompass both the future of the team and the future of the team's offerings. The four key elements of this vision should be:

1 the team's strategy;

2 an action plan for implementing the team's strategy;

3 business plans for developing new and existing offerings;

4 action plans for each offering.

You must provide the creative input to formulate this vision of the future, but I can help by providing a structure that ensures you consider many of the key questions that need answering. However, a word of warning, every strategy and plan will be unique, so be alert for issues that affect your team and its offerings, which are not highlighted by my generic template.

Developing a team strategy

I divide a strategy into eight different sections.

brilliant tip

Answer all the questions posed in these eight sections very quickly. You are looking for the 'aha!' moments when the question has helped you spot something that needs to be added to your SWOT (Stengths, Weaknesses, Opportunities and Threats) analysis, and that may need to be part of your strategy and/or action plan.

1 The current financial position

Using a maritime navigation analogy, your strategy can be considered as the way you plot the future course of your ship and whether you reach your intended destination. Obviously you cannot plot a course if you don't know where your current location is.

Do you understand what your current financial position really is? If you have recently taken over a team then there is a high probability that you do not understand the current position, and it is also quite likely that the previous team leader didn't understand it either. Even if you have been running your team for a while it is possible that you do not have an adequate understanding of your current situation.

> do you understand what your current financial position really is?

You should consider, at the very least, the following issues.

- What are all the revenue streams that generate the team's income? What do you know about the properties of those revenue streams: are they likely to continue into the future, are they likely to grow or decline, how predictable are they, what margin do they generate, etc.?

- What is your cost base? How is it structured? Which costs are fixed and which are variable? What services do you pay for from your parent organisation? Are there hidden costs which your organisation pays for that are not attributed to your team?

● How much profit did your team make last year? How much profit are you predicting for this year … and are you on target to achieve this profit? Is cash flow a major issue, if so, do you understand your cash flow?

● Do you know how much profit/loss each of your offerings are making? Loss-making offerings will need urgent attention.

● Who are your customers, what revenue do you expect to get from them this year, and how does this compare to revenue in past years?

Many of the remaining seven sections of the strategy will start with additional elements of your team's current position.

brilliant tip

Do not be surprised if your organisation's accounting system does not provide you with much data that is helpful in establishing your current financial position: it will have been set up to answer different questions. Most managers/leaders have to keep their own accounts.

2 The external environment

Using a sailing navigation analogy again, you cannot navigate without knowing about winds, currents and the roughness of the sea. You will also be very interested in weather forecasts and tide tables. Finally, you will also need good charts to spot sandbanks, reefs, etc. Failure to understand the external environment is an easy way to get shipwrecked … and the same is true for your team's journey into the future.

One of the easiest traps that a team can fall into is to become inward looking. A simple way to remind yourself of this danger is to remember that your customers are part of your external environment. Most of the risks that a strategy should try to manage will come from changes in the external market.

Your external environment includes at least:

- customers;
- competitors;
- suppliers;
- partners;
- stakeholders;
- the markets you sell into;
- the media;
- PEST – political, economic, social, and technological – factors.

You will also have important links to the external environment:

- product distribution channels, including sales people employed by your organisation;
- market and media research/analysts;
- PR agencies (inside and outside your organisation);
- advertising channels;
- your personal network of contacts.

I am sure you are very familiar with the concept of a SWOT analysis – strengths, weaknesses, opportunities and threats. It is well worth developing a SWOT analysis as you go through these eight sections of your strategy as it will form an important part of your written strategy. You will find that your analysis of the external environment will produce many strengths, weaknesses and threats. It will also hopefully point the way towards many of your opportunities.

Expanding now on the questions you need to ask yourself about the external factors and links mentioned above. Consider the following.

Customers

- How well do you know your customers? Do you understand your customers well enough to know if you can build more business with them, or are you defending your current level of business?

- Are you dependent on your customer relationships with any key individuals in the customer organisations or your own organisation?

- Have you applied Pareto's law and identified the top 20 per cent of your customers who probably provide 80 per cent of your revenue? Do you at least know the top 20 per cent of your customers well?

- Do you have a sufficient spread of customers to survive if you lose one or more of your best customers.

- Are there any customers who are so important that if you lost their business the future of your team is threatened? Do you know any such customers very well?

- Do you personally devote enough of your time to customer contact?

- Do you know what each of your customers thinks of your offerings and customer service?

- Are any of your customers more trouble than they are worth?

Competitors

I will deal with competitors in the next section of the strategy, *Market positioning*.

Suppliers

- Are there any of your suppliers that cannot be quickly and cost-effectively replaced?

- Could you make savings by renegotiating an existing supply contract, or changing suppliers?

- Are any of your team too close to any of your suppliers?

Partners

Partners are key when your team does not have all the capabilities to provide the solution that a customer buys, and you share some profit and risk with a partner rather than just buying in that capability from a supplier (internally or externally).

● Do you have a clear contract with your partner, which you are both happy with?

● Do you have a good understanding of your partner?

● Are your organisation and your partner's interests in good alignment?

● Is the balance of power between your organisations in reasonable balance, or is one party much more dependent on the relationship than the other? (Unbalanced power relationships are a risk.)

● Do you know what your partner thinks of your organisation and your team?

● Do you think your partner wishes to expand their business relationship with you?

● Is your relationship dependent on specific individuals?

Stakeholders

Stakeholders are all the people and organisations outside your team who feel they should have some control or influence over you, and who will feel that they should be appropriately consulted. For example, there will be numerous stakeholders within your own organisation. If you have invested a non-trivial amount of the organisation's money in a venture, then there are likely to be stakeholders who feel they have the right to check that you are using that investment wisely. As another example, if you have an important customer who relies heavily on your products or services, they will feel they are a stakeholder.

Sadly it is quite common for leaders to manage some of their stakeholders badly.

● Do you know who all your stakeholders are? Apply Pareto's law – and identify the 20 per cent of stakeholders who have the power to give you 80 per cent of the grief.

● Do you understand your stakeholders' interests appropriately?

● Are you investing enough of your time in talking to your stakeholders?

● Is your relationship with your stakeholders likely to change? If so, how?

● Are the risks of upsetting your stakeholders being managed properly?

The markets you sell into

This will be dealt with in the next section.

The media

This isn't just the printed and broadcast media, but increasingly covers the Internet. You will use the media to tell potential customers about your offerings, and as a source of market intelligence. The media can all be a source of negative publicity.

● Do you know about all the relevant media? Are you sure you know about all the relevant media?

● Do you have a process for tracking what is happening in the media that is relevant to your business?

● Do you have good links to your organisation's press and PR capabilities?

● Do you have a plan to exploit the media to tell potential customers about your offerings?

● Have you thought about the obvious ways that something could go wrong that could generate negative media comment (e.g. from your PEST analysis)? Is this a significant enough risk that you need contingency plans of how your organisation will respond?

PEST(EL) factors

PEST originally stood for political, economic, social and technological factors. More recently environmental and legal/ regulatory issues have been added to produce PESTEL or PESTL. While PESTEL factors are becoming ever more significant I won't cover them in great detail here because the issues you need to consider are quite complex and are well covered on the Web. When doing a PESTEL analysis it is well worth remembering the following.

- You need to think about these issues in any export markets or countries to which you outsource.
- Ensure that you cost PESTEL risks realistically ... too many managers just cross their fingers and hope.
- Technological issues, such as the Internet and mobile technology, are a game changer for many business opportunities.
- Mitigate legal and regulatory risks. For example, cutting corners on issues such as health and safety or pollution is not only immoral and illegal, but it is also very bad business. You need to understand the financial implications of such issues.

brilliant tip

One of the best defences against PESTEL issues is to ensure that you can respond quickly to changes and problems. Often PESTEL issues cannot be predicted, but the agile business is the one that will survive these risks.

Remember that fraud is a good way to a short-term profit … and a long-term relationship with a cell mate.

Product distribution channels

When an inferior product outsells a better product one frequently hears that the inferior product succeeded because of superior marketing. This is occasionally true, but much more likely is that the inferior product had much better distribution channels or was better priced. Time and again it is the distribution channel that is king.

> it is the distribution channel that is king

Designing an offering to take advantage of an existing distribution channel is often a very clever strategy – for example, if you design a product that your sales people could pitch alongside an existing successful product.

It is not unusual for there to be conflict between different distribution channels. A common example is when direct selling conflicts with external distribution channels. You need to ensure that the channels that deliver the most revenue are most protected.

You need to remember that if your distribution channel offers poor customer service then it is your reputation that may well suffer. This means you need to plan to have good visibility and sufficient control over your distribution channels to mitigate this risk.

If I had to single out the most common mistake in business strategies it would be to pay insufficient attention to distribution channels.

> ### brilliant tip
>
> Remember that your sales people want to earn commissions easily. You need to hand them an easy pitch, with clear customer benefits and clear differentiation from competitors. They will need good marketing and sales collateral, and good pre-sales support from your team. This really is the only way to have a good relationship with your sales force.

Market and media research/analysts

Everyone professes to know that knowledge is power. You need to assess how important it is to understand the market and the media; if it is not that important ... check again. External analysis and research can be important, but is seldom cheap, and there are plenty of second-rate services available. It is also essential that you make your own mind up and do not delegate too much of the task to external consultants. If you and/or your team are not on top of media and market monitoring and analysis then your SWOT analysis is unlikely to be accurate.

PR agencies

PR is usually vastly more cost-effective than advertising as a way of getting your offering known to potential customers. It can also be a major threat if the media pick up a negative story. If you have significant (positive or negative) PR potential then you need to plan to develop the best possible relationship with your organisation's PR professionals. Usually any links to external PR agencies will have to go through your internal PR people. Many organisations will not charge you directly for using your own PR staff, which makes them appear a 'free' resource.

> ## brilliant tip
>
> If your PR people do a good job, be sure to let their managers know. Not only is it polite, but if you make them look good, they will try even harder to give you a good service.

Advertising channels

Printed media advertising tends to be very expensive, and is largely the preserve of building brands. Internet advertising, especially through search engines can be much more effective, but you will need to constantly monitor it for cost-effectiveness. Generally PR is much better value for money than advertising.

Your personal network of contacts

I would certainly recommend that you invest in reading *Brilliant Networking* by Steven D'Souza. Few brilliant leaders do not have a brilliant personal network. Brilliant leaders are usually brilliant listeners, and that is an excellent start to building a personal network. Remember to be a giver of intelligence not just a taker.

3 Market positioning

A quick checklist.

- Do you know who all your competitors are?
- Do you know the strengths and weaknesses of your offering when compared to each competitor's?
- Do you know what prices your competitors charge, and how they structure their pricing?
- Do you have any USPs – unique selling points?

- Do you know how you could take customers from your competitors (and vice versa)?

- Does your sales and marketing collateral clearly tell customers how they will benefit, and why your offerings are better than your competitors'?

- Do you have good customer references, case studies and press comments?

- How do your distribution channels compare to your competitors'?

- Do you understand who your customers are?

- Do you know how your customers perceive your offerings and customer care?

- Do your offerings have clear, strong brands?

- Are there likely to be more or fewer customers in future?

- Are there customers you don't currently sell to who would buy the current or an adapted offering?

- Do your customers have to buy your offering, or is it a discretionary purchase? If it is discretionary, do you have a plan for surviving a recession?

- Do you know who makes the purchasing decisions, and how you can reach them directly?

- What are the properties of the market you sell into?
  - Is it a market niche or mainstream?
  - If a market is niche, are there any related niche markets you could target?
  - Is the market still growing or is it declining?
  - If the market is growing, when might it reach saturation and start declining? Are you growing capacity that may not be needed in the future?
  - Are you selling into an early market? If so how will you move from selling to early adopters to more mainstream (conservative) customers?

- If a market is mature is it likely that it will consolidate to fewer, larger suppliers, and how might this impact on your strategy?
- If a market is declining are alternative products being purchased, and do these offer opportunities to you?
- Will specialist products be displaced by commoditised products and services?
- How price-sensitive is the market?
- Do you expect prices to rise or fall in your market?
- Are there any external factors that could rapidly destabilise your market?
- How is your market being affected by the Internet (not forgetting the rapid rise of the mobile Internet)?

brilliant example

As an example of the importance of spotting that a market might saturate, consider the cruising business. Lots of new cruise ships are being built to satisfy the growing demand for cruises. Eventually the market will saturate and as new ships become available there will be an oversupply of cruise liners. Prices will then drop significantly and a lot of cruise operators will go to the wall.

One of the most important parts of your strategy is to decide how you want to evolve your portfolio of offerings.

The first place to start is to decide whether you wish to close down any of your offerings. It is surprising how frequently this question isn't seriously considered. Then you want to consider how you can make more of your existing

> decide whether you wish to close down any of your offerings

offerings. Hopefully you have business plans for your offerings (as described later). These need reviewing when you write or update your strategy. For each offering you need to consider at least the following.

● Does it need refreshing?

● Do you need to improve your distribution channels?

● Does after sales and/or customer service need improving?

● Would better marketing produce enough extra sales to justify the extra marketing spend?

● Can you reduce costs?

● Can you grow the number of customers, and/or the spend per customer?

You then need to consider the possibility of incremental offerings that build on an existing offering to produce extra sales to existing customers and/or can be sold to new customers. You need to prepare business plans for those that appear most attractive.

brilliant tip

Your whole team needs to be aware of the need to spot potential new offerings and to let you know of any ideas they have.

Although they are quite unusual, you need to be be alert to the possibility of completely new offerings. Sometimes you might be asked to do some bespoke work for a customer, and this can be a good way to jump-start such offerings. You also need to use your knowledge of market trends, and your understanding of your team's capabilities to try and spot potential new offerings.

brilliant tip

When considering any changes/additions to your offerings you
need to be aware of what investment funds may be available to
you, and to prioritise those that offer the best return.

Does your team, as opposed to your offerings, need to have a
strong brand and be marketed to your customers? Many teams
rely solely on marketing and brands for their offerings, but large
stable teams may well want to build up a team brand ... in which
case you need to have a credible, affordable marketing strategy. I
have found *Brilliant Marketing* by Richard Hall, to be one of the
best books available to understand marketing issues

4 Managing your cost base

Thinking up new opportunities is exciting, whereas cutting costs
is dull, dull, dull. Guess which most leaders/managers give priority to? Every penny you cut goes straight on the bottom line.
Cutting costs is usually lower risk than investing in new opportunities. In terms of a quick win, cutting your cost base should
often be top of the list.

Yet another checklist.

● Bureaucracy costs money and stifles agility; cut all non-
  essential bureaucracy.

● Do you have the right organisational structure? Can anyone
  who is not contributing to the bottom line be moved to
  revenue-generating work?

● You will have already thought about cutting costs by
  instituting better processes for maintaining, developing and
  supporting your offerings. Can you streamline your team's
  processes?

- Can staff productivity be improved?
- Are your team fully motivated?
- Do your team behave in ways that maximise the team's profit? For example, do they all behave in a flexible way?
- Are there any conventional cost-saving measures you could implement to cut overheads, such as the travel budget, accommodation costs, IT costs, support costs, suppliers' costs, etc.?
- Do you have the right performance metrics?
- Do you have the right staff incentives?
- Are you providing services to other parts of the organisation that you should be paid for?

brilliant tip

You can often make significant savings by renegotiating, or re-competing, supply contracts.

5 Your assets/capabilities

You need to analyse your assets.

- Do you know your staff's capabilities?
- Are your people doing jobs that play to their strengths?
- Are your key staff being used to the best effect?
- Are you very dependent on any key staff? What would you do if they left? Have you done adequate succession planning?
- Review the team's track record: what do you know how to do?
- Do you have any valuable intellectual property rights (IPRs), copyrighted material and know-how?

- Do you have any significant equipment or other physical assets?
- Do you have access to major capabilities, such as a 24/7 call or operations centre, or are there capabilities you need access to?
- Do you have any major sources of repeating revenue?

Other assets will have been analysed in earlier sections, such as market intelligence, distribution channels, brands, etc.

6 Constraints

You must develop a strategy that works within the constraints that apply to your team, such as the following.

- What higher-level organisational strategies apply to you?
- What important organisational initiatives are ongoing, or are likely to be introduced?
- Do you understand the relevant organisational politics?
- What investment funds can you get access to?
- Can you expand or decrease your staff numbers?
- Do your offerings fit well with your organisation's brand and market position?

7 SWOT

Create your SWOT analysis from the first six sections. Once you have created a draft strategy in section 8 you need to add the risks of implementing this strategy to your SWOT.

brilliant tip

Concentrate on only the most important strengths, weaknesses, opportunities and threats.

8 Your strategy

Creating a strategy is a highly iterative process, but you eventually need to capture the key changes that you wish to make in the near, medium and (occasionally) long term. The important changes are:

● improving and extending your offerings;

● implementing cost savings;

● mitigating risks/threats;

● developing new assets and capabilities.

The late Sir John Harvey-Jones identified an important class of changes, which he referred to as 'catalytic'. Catalytic changes are those that initiate major changes in behaviours. Such changes can be either very good or very bad. Changing metrics and incentives often lead to catalytic changes. I have also seen the genuine delegation of authority and responsibility produce such catalytic effects. Disseminating key business performance information is yet another source of catalytic changes. Catalytic changes are often very inexpensive to implement.

> catalytic changes are often very inexpensive to implement

brilliant tip

Your strategy needs to be consistent with the amount of investment and management time available to implement it.

You need to write your strategy down and you need to worry if it is more than four pages long. Having done this, you may be able to extract a short, useful vision statement. A good vision statement can become a vital focal point for your team. However it is better to have no vision statement than it is to have an anodyne, inaccurate or rambling statement.

brilliant tip

Put an early draft of your strategy out for review by your team and capture their inputs. Before finalising your strategy show it to your bosses and get their comments.

Developing a strategy action plan

At first sight you might well think that without an action plan your strategy will be of no use. In fact a key part of a strategy's value is to allow you to react appropriately to events and opportunities as they arise. For example, an event highlighted in the press might present a chance to pursue part of your strategy. An invitation to tender for a new contract might allow you to develop a capability and track record in an area highlighted by your strategy. If you know where you want your business to go in the future, then it is very likely you will react much more intelligently to future, unpredictable events.

When drawing up an action plan, you must remember that you are likely only to have the resources (time and money) to do a few things at any one time. It is also likely that you want to include some quick wins, so that the team can see that they are making progress. You also may want to leave sufficient slack in order to respond to opportunities that happen to arise.

brilliant tip

It makes obvious sense to prioritise actions that provide the best value for money.

Try to avoid your busy schedule becoming a bottleneck, and remember that an action that can be delegated may take precedence over an action that only you can implement.

I would recommend seeking feedback from your team about the design of an action plan. This will help you avoid favouring your pet projects. Consultation will also help get buy-in from the team. When executing your action plan, review whether progress of actions is satisfactory. If it isn't, do you need to just try harder, modify your plan, or even abandon some actions? Remember your action plan is your servant, not your master. However, it is your personal responsibility to maintain momentum in implementing change.

seek feedback about the design of an action plan

Developing a business plan

Business plans are traditionally viewed as the written proposition to gain investment funding. This means that they are usually slanted to present a sufficiently rosy view to gain the funding required. What I will do in this section is show you how to prepare a real business plan, from which you will easily be able to generate plans in whatever format, for whatever purpose, you require.

The problem with my approach is that it is honest, and if you are honest then many business propositions will not look sufficiently attractive to invest in. The thing you have to remember is that the biggest risk is nearly always the risk you haven't thought of; but likewise the biggest opportunity is frequently the one you didn't think of … and if you never do anything you will never find these unanticipated lucky breaks. For this reason I would recommend:

- do things fast;
- do them economically;

- start many cheap things in preference to a few expensive opportunities;

- do things flexibly so you can pursue any lucky breaks;

- make sure you can abandon an opportunity cheaply;

- stop pursuing an opportunity as soon as you see it is likely to fail;

- once it is clear you are on to a winner, secure appropriate additional investment to build a long-lasting, highly profitable business.

Many of these ideas are expanded upon in Chapter 7, *Brilliant business tips*.

brilliant tip

Before starting your business plan, check that the proposed offering is a good match for your organisation's brand. If your organisation wouldn't obviously sell the offering then it is very unlikely that it will invest in developing it for the market.

The following ten sections outline a good generic structure for a business plan.

1 How compelling is your proposition?

It is very easy to fool yourself that the world will beat a path to your door to buy your offering. You really need to understand why a customer **needs** to buy your offering. And I do mean **needs** … just gaining some benefits is seldom enough. If a product solves one of a customer's top three problems then you are off to a good start. Here are some other good tests to apply.

- Can you tell a customer why they should buy it in less than a minute (a compelling elevator pitch)?

- Is the customer buying it likely to have the budgetary authority to buy it?

- Will the customers easily believe that they will get a quick return on investment from buying and deploying the offering? This is key to being able to sell to conservative customers.

- Is the offering very easy to deploy, or does it require a significant change to the customer's current working practices?

- Is your offering clearly differentiated in features or price from your competitors'?

2 Understanding the market

Answer the following questions.

- How big is the potential market?
- Who are your competitors?
- Why will customers buy from you rather than a competitor?
- How mature is the market?
- How long is the market likely to last?
- Is the market likely to consolidate into fewer, larger players? How will you cope with such consolidation?
- How are prices likely to change in the market in the future?
- Do you face any discontinuities, such as moving from an early adopter market to a mainstream market? How will you cope with such discontinuities?

You should attempt to make a first estimate of likely sales projections over the coming five years.

brilliant tip

Having a superior or cheaper offering is good, but nothing beats the quality of your distribution channels.

3 Your marketing strategy

It is no good having a compelling proposition if your potential customers are unaware of it.

Access to existing channels to market is the best solution. See the *Distribution channels* section below for the issues to consider if you don't have ready-made channels to market.

Other issues to consider are the following.

- PR – usually cheaper than advertising … but is your offering newsworthy? Does your organisation have a good PR/press office to help you?
- Advertising – do your customers read a particular publication, and can you afford to advertise in it? Can you advertise cost-effectively on a search engine?
- Direct mail shot (paper or electronic) – can you get access to a good mailing list?
- Can you partner with an organisation that has a relationship with your potential customers?
- You will almost certainly need a good website, and you will probably need to work with whoever controls the online presence of your organisation.

4 Distribution channels

Who will sell your offering to potential customers? Do you have access to a direct sales force in your organisation? Are your sales people already selling other offerings that would allow them to pitch your offering on the same sales visits? Does your organisation have existing external distribution channels who would be interested in handling your offering?

brilliant tip

Don't assume that an existing sales force or distribution channel will necessarily be interested in adding your offering to their portfolio … they will only be interested in you if you can make them a substantial amount of money. You must engage with them early, and listen carefully to their feedback on your offering. You have to sell to the sellers.

If you don't have ready-made channels then unless you can come up with a credible distribution model, your offering isn't worth pursuing. Don't underestimate how difficult and potentially risky it is to build up a new distribution network from scratch.

● Hiring new sales people is costly, and what will you do with them if the offering fails?

● Hiring in freelance sales people is very expensive, but presents fewer long-term risks. They also tend to be very motivated. You can also hire in freelance sales people with specific market knowledge.

● Your team will have in-depth knowledge of the offering and you need to budget for a significant amount of their time helping the sales process.

● Creating a new indirect channel network will be very challenging. I suggest you prepare draft marketing collateral and explore potential distributors and value added resellers before you invest heavily in an offering.

● Direct sales via the Internet can be a lifesaver for many new business offerings. It is likely your organisation already has an existing infrastructure to support online selling, and you need to check how you can get access to this infrastructure. You will need to sell your offering to those who control your organisation's online presence.

At the risk of boring you I will repeat:

The distribution channel is king.

▶ brilliant example

As an author I would like to think that *Brilliant Manager* has become an international bestseller because I wrote it so well. Writing a good book was necessary but not sufficient. It was my publisher's world-class sales force, marketing, and foreign rights department that were also responsible for this book's sales success.

---

5 Partners and suppliers

Few offerings can, or should be, totally an in-house effort. Does your customer need to purchase other products to gain full benefits from your offering? Should you be buying in parts of your offering rather developing them all in-house? Can you find appropriate suppliers and partners?

6 Support issues

We are now getting to the sections of a business plan that are typically skimped on.

How will you support your customers? If you depend on a 'wing and a prayer' you may well get away with it while you test your business offering in the marketplace. Once it is clear that the business is viable, you will need to put in place proper support processes ...

> How will you support your customers?

and these are seldom cheap. Almost every business plan I have seen vastly underestimated support costs and warranty claims.

7 Risks

I mentioned earlier that the biggest risk is nearly always the one you didn't think of. This means that you should allow a significant contingency in your costings for unanticipated risks ... although I have never seen a business plan that did this.

Every risk register is going to be unique, but some generic items to consider are:

- overruns in product development;
- higher than expected warranty costs;
- being sued;
- being prosecuted;
- attracting negative publicity;
- having to close down an offering that has attracted an uneconomic number of customers who will need continued support;
- losing key staff;
- environmental problems, from weather, fire, volcanic ash clouds, etc.;
- lack of prior experience – if you haven't done something like this before, your risks go through the roof;
- loss of a senior advocate for your offering within your organisation;
- loss of partners or suppliers;
- a new competitor with a better brand or channels to market, who brings out a similar product and takes your hard-won market share away from you.

You should cost each of these risks, for example by taking out insurance ... but if you do this realistically, you might not get investment funding.

8 Opportunities

Just as risks cannot always be anticipated, opportunities often turn up unexpectedly. However you should analyse whether this offering has a high, medium or low probability of leading on to other offerings. Questions to ask yourself are these.

- If you are targeting a niche market, could you extend the offering into other niches?
- Are there obvious follow-on offerings if it is a success?
- Are you creating any infrastructure that could be reused?
- Are you generating know-how that might be applied elsewhere?
- Will you be creating relationships with new customers who could be sold other offerings?
- Will you be creating a brand that could be stretched?

9 Cost model

You need to estimate investment costs prior to launch. Then estimate fixed and variable running costs. Work out the marginal cost of servicing a new customer. Work out if additional investment could reduce marginal costs, which will help you decide if, or when, it is worth investing to improve the scalability of your offering.

Remember to cost:

- risks, including contingency;
- maintaining the knowledge base to support the offering;
- support costs;
- supplier costs;
- marketing costs;
- sales costs;
- regularly refreshing the offering and the offering's infrastructure;

- future investments to reduce recurring costs, to handle increased demand, and/or increase quality;
- warranty costs;
- depreciation of equipment;
- inflation;
- etc.

brilliant tip

At the very least, get an accountant to run their eyes over your figures.

10 Revenue model

Estimate how price-sensitive your market is; know what your competitors are charging; then work out a pricing structure. Plug in your market projections; make a best guess optimisation of price versus volume … and then run the numbers. You can then work out break-even points, margins and estimated profits/losses for your plan. The most important output is your sales targets for the coming year. If you think these are too challenging, then you may want to forget pursuing this offering.

> the most important output is your sales targets for the coming year

Many managers who work in large organisations are shielded from the full horror of cash flow issues. If cash flow is a significant issue for you then this is the place to plan how you will maintain cash flow.

You will now be in a good position to write your business plan in whatever format it is requested.

Developing a business opportunity action plan

You now need to decide how and when you will seek investment funding. Plan when and how to develop the offering, marketing plan, support infrastructure ... and all the other aspects of your (honest) business plan.

brilliant tip

Remember to build lots of contingency into your timetable ... then run like hell to beat your deadlines.

Summary

I have provided templates for business strategies and business plans. I have also provided detailed checklists to go through that will help you identify many of the key issues. Go through these checklists quickly to spot what is important to you. You and your team members then need to be both creative and analytical to create good strategies and plans. Good luck ... and I promise you it is worth the effort.

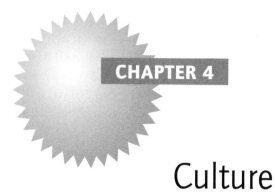

CHAPTER 4

Culture

One of the signs that you are getting it right as a manager is when your team behaves as you want without being supervised or explicitly instructed to do so. A strongly defined culture within the team is an excellent way of achieving this desirable state. If team members instinctively know 'this is the way we do things' and 'we don't do things like that' then team members will tend to act in ways you approve of, and avoid doing things you would disapprove of. More than that, there will be peer pressure within the team for everyone to behave in ways that are compatible with the team culture. Another desirable consequence of the team culture reinforcing your own principles is that team members will be able to easily predict how you would react to a particular set of circumstances. Hearing someone say 'I knew you would do that' is not an indication that you are unimaginative and dull, but should be taken as a compliment of the highest order.

So how do you achieve a good, strong culture? Reiterating the golden rule of management in a slightly different form:

Consistent behaviour by the leader sets the tone for the culture.

I have included the word *consistent* to stress that inconsistent behaviour will very rapidly produce a dysfunctional culture. Almost as bad will be if your words and your actions are inconsistent – in such cases your actions will set the culture, but your personal standing will be severely undermined.

Understand the existing culture

The chances are that you took over the running of an existing team. You need to understand what culture you have inherited and, in particular, what aspects of the culture are highly valued by your staff. Changing any aspect of the existing culture will need skilful and honest handling. Generally speaking, a wise new manager takes their time to understand a new team and avoids rapid changes of direction. A second influence on your team's culture will be if your organisation has strong cultural traits. For example, if you work for an aggressive and combative organisation, you will have difficulty if you try to create a culture that runs directly counter to this organisational bias.

I will split the remainder of the chapter into two parts. The first will be a discussion of the different sorts of culture that you may want to create. The second part will discuss what techniques you can deploy to change the culture in the directions that you want – or, alternatively, that will change the culture in ways you may not want if you do not plan your behaviour appropriately.

What sort of culture do you want?

As this book is aimed at the managers of the value creation within an organisation, or those who provide a service to others who create value, many of your team will deal with customers within or outside the organisation. If this is the case I strongly suggest you have strong cultural values about customer service. In the section on how to create a culture I will return to customer service as an example.

Many strong cultures have extreme aspects to them. I want to use this as an example of a common fallacy. A culture is a social system, and any soft science that grows up around such complex systems – be it management science, psychology or economics – is very prone to incorrect suppositions of cause and effect. The fact that strong cultures are usually extreme does not imply that by making a culture extreme you will necessarily make it strong. Other examples might be: (from economics) strong economies have stable exchange rates, but forcing an exchange rate to be stable will not necessarily produce a strong economy; or (from management theory) good companies nearly always have good quality systems, but implementing a good quality system will not necessarily significantly improve your company. On the subject of extremism in cultures, all I would say is don't be afraid of making the culture extreme in pursuit of a principle you feel very strongly about. However, a word of warning: I

> don't be afraid of making the culture extreme

know of very few cultures that have numerous, different extreme aspects. You will have to be highly selective about those aspects of the culture you choose to highlight in an extreme fashion.

I am suggesting that you should align the culture with your leadership principles. You will also want to consider aligning the culture to reinforce other key aspects of your management

Many strong cultures have extreme aspects to them

approach. In managing aspects of your business, for example customer service or the financial bottom line, you will probably have to adopt a technique described in *management-speak* as *loose/tight*. All this means is that you choose a few key factors to control tightly and will leave all the other factors under much looser control. As an example, consider the financial controls within your organisation – I will bet that you can instantly identify the tight financial controls, be it capital expenditure or cash flow or staff utilisation or margins or volume. You should consider which tight controls you exercise within your team are naturally suited to cultural reinforcement.

brilliant tip

Focus on important cultural issues. Changing a culture is a slow and difficult business. Don't waste your time trying to change aspects of a culture that you dislike but which don't make a major difference to the bottom line. By following the golden rule you may well slowly change the aspects you dislike anyway.

Few teams today are insulated from the need to constantly explore changes to their current operations. To encourage this you will have to develop a culture that *genuinely* tolerates honourable failure. This fact is constantly stressed by management gurus and most organisations pay lip service to this idea ... but their actions usually betray the shallowness of their understanding of the concept of tolerating failure. Within the more narrow confines of your team you must ensure that those who fail honourably are not penalised and, if appropriate, are rewarded on pay, promotion or other tangible aspects of their careers.

Many strong cultures think of themselves as an elite. This can be a valuable attitude as it means that the culture sets itself very high standards, which will naturally tend to lead to high-quality outputs from your team. There is, however, a less positive side. Elites tend to be very insular and often regard those outside their culture as 'useless' or 'stupid'. The view of an elite from the outside often calls them 'arrogant' and 'overbearing'. By ensuring that your personal behaviour is always tolerant and respectful of people outside the culture, and by going out of your way to show you disapprove of intolerance to outsiders, you can go a long way to counteracting this natural tendency.

How to create and change a culture

How you use your own time

An implication of the golden rule is that what you spend your time doing will send a very strong message to the team about your priorities. As an example I will describe a common mistake I see time and again. Managers often involve themselves in the pursuit of new business opportunities. There is nothing wrong in this, but if it gets to the stage that you spend little or no time taking an interest in your team's existing core business and its customers, then you can expect those working to generate the bulk of your income to feel thoroughly unappreciated.

Management processes

One of the most important tools you have at your disposal is the detailed design of the processes within your team. Changing processes can have a major impact on the culture. I will use a business-related example concerning the team's attitude to customer service. Consider the impact that allowing staff who interact directly with customers to have delegated authority to resolve some customer complaints 'on the spot' without reference to you or anyone else in authority. Do you trust your staff with such authority? Just how much authority are you willing to delegate? Do you think you need additional processes to manage the risk that the delegated authority will be mistakenly applied? Are your staff sufficiently aware of the big picture to exercise such authority properly? Are they sufficiently well trained to exercise such authority safely? All these issues will lead to the team members being aware of the level to which they personally are responsible for customer satisfaction, and this will quickly become ingrained as part of the cultural approach to customer service. Although this is a somewhat simplistic example it hopefully illustrates the key role that processes can play in defining the team culture.

Pay and promotion

Your implementation of staff pay and promotions will seriously impact on the culture of your team. You are bound to be constrained by organisational processes, but you must remember the fundamental rule of staff dissatisfaction:

Your staff will be most affected by comparison with other team members, secondly by others in the organisation, and lastly by comparison with others outside the organisation.

You must ensure you treat your staff in an appropriately open and fair way when it comes to pay, promotions and bonuses. Just one bad promotion decision can have a serious impact on your credibility and a major impact on staff morale – make sure you get it right! Time invested in getting it right is time well spent. Resist the temptation to use promotions and bonuses to reward those working on your current favourite projects – everyone must be treated equally. One useful way of avoiding promoting the wrong people is to bounce your ideas for future promotions off a few of the experienced members of your team.

I offer much more detailed advice in Chapter 10, *Management master-class*.

Recruitment

Another area I would encourage you to invest your own time in is recruitment. The sorts of staff you are trying to recruit sends a very strong message to the team. Your personal involvement will also show that you take a personal interest in the future of the team. It is also the key to the level of diversity you want the culture to tolerate. A common failing of the strong leader is to recruit clones of themselves, which reinforces the fact that the culture will tend to absorb the leader's failings anyway. As an example, consider your current staff and think which of them are best suited to starting with a project, those that are good at working on a mature project, and those that are good at finishing things off. Finishers are a rare breed and tend to be unflashy personalities. It is your job to ensure that you get an appropriately broad mix of staff into the team. A second word of warning is to ensure that you do not allow any feelings of insecurity to discourage the recruitment of outstanding staff – you must not view such staff as a threat. Just remember that good people recruit better people, while poor people recruit worse people.

> finishers are a rare breed and tend to be unflashy personalities

Recruitment is an interesting example of how cultures can become self-perpetuating. A strongly defined culture will be attractive to like-minded recruits and will tend to repel those who would not fit in. If someone is recruited who does not fit in then a strong culture tends to expel them – not physically, but someone who does not fit in will tend not to thrive and not be really happy in the team, and will often leave of their own accord.

brilliant tip

A poorly written and constructed CV often means a poor candidate.

When designing your recruitment process the following points are worthy of consideration.

● Think carefully about the qualities and skills you are

looking for and ensure that your recruitment process tests candidates for those qualities and skills.

- A full day is about the correct length of time for the initial selection process, although you may ask those that have done well, but you are not sure about, to come back for another visit.

- Hold the selection day in your normal working environment and expose the candidates to the team culture.

- Use the formal interview to test for the person's qualities (personality, motivations, judgement and ethics), not their professional expertise. An excellent technique is to ask the candidates to illustrate their answers from their own past experiences – 'Can you give me an example of how you handled a difficult person who was in authority over you?'

- Use an informal interview to probe their professional expertise and experience.

- Ask candidates to bring examples of previous work. How many times have I seen programmers being hired by organisations that have not seen one line of a program written by the person?

- Ask the person to prepare a 10-minute presentation on some experience, within a work context, they found interesting. Have a small group from your team spend 10 or 15 minutes asking them questions on their presentation.

- Have a short (about 30 minutes) practical test. I have used a short case study that asked the candidate to analyse a fairly general work-related problem.

- Make sure the recruit has a one-to-one with a fairly new team member where the recruit can quiz them.

Try to handle the process as informally as possible. You want to find out about the recruit, and for the recruit to decide if they like your team. There is no reason it cannot be an enjoyable experience for the recruit – if it is fun they are much more likely to accept a job offer.

Staff retention

Retaining the staff you recruit, especially the best staff, is obviously as important as recruiting staff in the first place. Many managers underestimate the financial cost of high staff turnover. A strong culture can have a dramatic, positive effect on staff retention. Industrial psychologists have long recognised that workers are motivated by an environment that gives their working life meaning. We are also motivated by the need to feel a sense of belonging. This may all sound a bit spiritual but these are powerful forces that can generate great staff loyalty. Anyone who has earned a position of respect within a strong culture will think long and hard before giving that up to move to a new job where they will have to rebuild such a position from scratch.

Physical surroundings

The effect of physical surroundings is often underrated by managers. Although you will often be severely constrained by your organisation's policies on accommodation, it is likely you can find significant 'wiggle room' to adapt the surroundings to better suit the culture you want. Maybe it is a reorganisation of an open-plan office area, or maybe an informal meeting area for coffee times, or the allocation of rooms for impromptu meetings. One reason that office accommodation raises such high passions is that workers understand how important it is to their efficiency and happiness – it is a pity that more managers and organisations do not understand this as passionately.

Staying on the subject of accommodation, your personal accommodation can present problems. For example, if your team works in open plan and you have a separate office, what message does this send to the team? The problem is that it is very difficult to be a good manager and leader without the confidentiality that comes from a separate office. If a separate office is available I recommend you accept it. If you are required to work in open plan then make sure that confidential conversations on the phone and one-to-one take place somewhere where you will have privacy.

brilliant example

There is a (possibly apocryphal) story about a new chief executive at Hewlett-Packard arriving at his new office, and his first action was unscrewing the door and leaving it propped up against the wall. The number of times I have heard this story told is testament to the significance that physical surroundings have on a culture. The story is also a good example of how what management gurus refer to as *myths and legends* are a powerful way in which cultures become self-sustaining. As new members of the culture hear such anecdotes they receive a powerful message about the underlying principles of the culture.

Social events

A rich source of myths and legends, usually of the embarrassing kind, is team social events. The social dimension is one that must be adapted to the individual circumstances of any particular team. The only suggestion I have to offer is that if you receive a bonus based on the performance of the team, you invest part of that bonus in sponsoring some team social events.

A plea for intolerance

I will conclude this section with an unusual plea for intolerance. I suggest you are extremely intolerant of anyone who breaks the fundamental *principles* of the culture. For example, if integrity is a cornerstone of the culture then those who play fast and loose with integrity should be nailed to the wall as an example to others.

I also suggest that you avoid the temptation to turn a blind eye to minor transgressions, such as bending the rules on expenses, minor health and safety infractions and bad-taste jokes. One of the reasons that a manager cannot be 'one of the gang' is that the leader of the culture should set high standards, both in their own behaviour and by reacting each and every time they find team members bending the rules.

the leader of the culture should set high standards

Summary

The principle that underlies the culture of your team is:

Consistent behaviour by the leader sets the tone for the culture.

Your actions will tell the team what you approve of and what you disapprove of.

You need to be aware of the impact that the subtle signals you send will have on your team's culture. Issues such as your office accommodation, how you prioritise your time and how you react to bad news will have a significant effect on the culture of your team.

Suggested reading

DeMarco, Tom and Timothy Lister (1999), *Peopleware: Productive Projects and Teams*, 2nd edn. New York, Dorset House.

    A provocative study of productivity in the software industry. It has the best, and most amusing, discussion of the effects of office accommodation on productivity that I have read.

Peters, Thomas and Robert H. Waterman (1998), *In Search of Excellence: Lessons from America's Best-Run Companies*. London, Warner Books.

    Similar in scope to *Built to Last*. First published in 1982, this is a famous management book. The examples are now very dated, but the underlying analysis of company cultures is still relevant.

CHAPTER 5

Managing different types of people

Shouldn't a manager treat everyone the same? Your innate sense of decency and fairness will push you in this direction but over time I have come to realise that a brilliant manager needs to understand the particular characteristics and hang-ups of different professions.

In this chapter I will be looking at a number of different professions and analysing what makes people who do these jobs tick. I will describe a number of techniques for having a good managerial relationship with these different professions, from very specific professions such as lawyers and software engineers, to more generic types such as support staff, sales people and creative people.

Before getting down to the details of the different types of people you have to manage and interact with, here are some fundamental principles that apply across the board.

When dealing with other professions, you need to respect their professionalism. There is absolutely no point in consulting a lawyer and then constantly arguing with them or ignoring their advice. On the other hand, professionals can often forget that their principal role is to *support* the manager in making a decision. In many cases it will be you who has to make the decision on business grounds, and it is for your experts to advise you of different possibilities and relevant implications. For example, if a creative person proposes a new product idea then you will probably have to take the lead in exploring how their idea could be adapted to bring it to market; you will pose market scenarios, but the creative person will be the one who knows best how to adapt their idea to those scenarios.

Interacting with people who are experts in different areas from yourself is a bit of an art. Here are the key points to remember.

Never show disrespect for an expert's professionalism

Many experts can try the patience of a saint! No matter how annoyed you get, you must never make the mistake of allowing your annoyance to be expressed in a disrespectful manner. For many experts, the worst of all insults is to accuse them of being unprofessional.

Do not allow yourself to be blinded by jargon

The best professionals can make themselves understood to laymen. There is a very common tendency for experts to hide behind a veneer of 'professional mystique'. Do not allow your experts to intimidate you. It is not only acceptable, it is essential that you require that experts explain their points to you in language that you can understand. If this means asking question after question after question – so be it. They will eventually get the message that you insist on understanding the issues that are relevant to the decisions you have to take.

> do not allow your experts to intimidate you

Explain your problems to your experts

I have found that it is nearly always very productive for you to explain your problem area to your experts. It is obviously much easier for them to help you if they understand the nature of the problems you face. Experts are usually fascinated to find out how your business works. I would, however, remind you that you should not use jargon on them!

Beware of advocacy

Experts have a nasty habit of holding strong, and not entirely rational, views on some areas of their expertise. If you detect the gleam of religious fervour in your adviser's eyes then you need to be on your guard. This is one of those times when you may need to seek a second opinion.

Beware the trendy solution

Another nasty habit of various professions is to follow the latest fad. You only have to look at your own area of management to see how many managers slavishly adopt the latest quack nostrum peddled by some management guru. If you suspect this effect, ask how well established the technique is, and ask for examples of the successful use of the solution proposed.

Be suspicious when told something is impossible

Experts will seldom tell you an outright lie. However, when they say, correctly, that something is impossible, they may well know that if you changed the question slightly then you could achieve what you wanted. This is why it is so important to explore the underlying issues and not to let your experts get you bogged down in irrelevant detail. A good question to ask is, 'Is there anything I can do that will give me 80 per cent of what I want?'

Beware of self-serving advice

I have done some management consultancy in my career, so I know how difficult it is to resist the temptation to recommend that an issue needs 'further study'. It is natural for experts to want you to become dependent on their advice. Given human nature, you must take the lead in ensuring that you get the advice that is the best for you, not the best for your advisers.

Beware of advisers withholding relevant information from you

Some experts seem to work on the basis that knowledge is power, and will attempt to ration the information they give you.

It is clear from the above how careful you have to be when dealing with expert advisers; so what can you do to get the best from them? There is one key technique that the brilliant manager should always fall back on – *keep asking questions until you fully understand the issues*. Use your advisers to inform you of the relevant issues. Certainly they can offer advice on your decision, but make it clear that you make the decisions – not them.

Enough of generalities, let's get down to some detail. There is a danger in the sections that follow that you will feel that I am guilty of perpetuating offensive stereotypes about different professions. I will try to avoid being offensive, but it is my view that many professions do indeed exhibit stereotypical characteristics. I am not saying that every member of every profession displays the qualities I describe, but I think that managers can benefit from being aware of how and why different professions tend to act, and react, in particular ways. I would also point out in my defence that in my career I have at various times been a creative type, an IT person, a salesman and also a consultant – so if I am insulting such people I am also insulting myself.

brilliant tip

Legal issues **really** matter. You ignore legal issues at your peril. If you need to deal with contracts, other legal agreements, or litigation, then you must listen carefully to your lawyers.

Lawyers

I will start with a confession – I have greatly enjoyed my interactions with my legal experts and contracts staff and I find the law a fascinating subject. So let me start by giving their side of the story.

First off, why do people always leave it too late to consult their lawyers? If only people asked for advice in good time then life would be so much easier. Second, no one remembers the pressure the lawyer was put under to get a contract out quickly when, years later, the agreement is tested in court and found to be poorly drafted. Third, people do not understand the importance of legal issues and tend to treat lawyers as an irritating nuisance who stop them getting on with their business, rather than experts who are trying to stop the careless manager from unnecessarily risking their business. I will spare you clauses IV to XXXII of the 'lament of the lawyer', but hopefully you recognise that there is at least some truth in the three gripes I have listed. So, why is there

> personality traits of managers and lawyers tend to be diametrically opposed

often such a frosty relationship between the manager/business person and the lawyer? The principal reason is that the fundamental personality traits of managers and lawyers tend to be diametrically opposed.

Managers tend to be risk-takers, while lawyers are trained to be risk-averse

I believe that managers and lawyers should openly acknowledge this fundamental divide and both sides should try to appreciate the views of the other side. The middle ground is *risk management* – your lawyer must ensure that you understand the full implications of all the risks you choose to accept.

An additional personality issue that managers need to be aware of is that *legal training reinforces adversarial personalities*. Lawyers are trained to win arguments, and so you need to be aware that most good lawyers enjoy a good fight – not to mention the fact that a good fight is usually highly profitable for lawyers.

I will finish this section with what you need to know, do and say to interact successfully with lawyers.

Lawyers seldom give short answers to questions

I have noticed that when lawyers answer a question they will frequently give a very full context to their answer, sometimes going all the way back to first principles. It is my experience that it is hopeless to resist and it is much better to listen patiently – you may even learn something new.

Don't involve lawyers directly in the early stages of business negotiations

The purpose of a legal agreement is to accurately record a deal that has been negotiated by business people. Lawyers do not have the right motivations, or the right temperaments, for business negotiations.

Regard contracts as prenuptials

One of the main services that lawyers provide is to help agree the divorce terms while both parties are still friends.

Don't let lawyers stop you handling a crisis properly

Of all the times I have found lawyers to be unhelpful, the most extreme is when there is a crisis. Lawyers, by their nature and training, like to fully research a topic before offering advice; so they react badly to having to give the snap advice needed in a crisis. A second major problem is that a crisis can often be best resolved, from a public relations perspective, by an honest admission of responsibility. Lawyers hate their clients admitting liability and, consequently, a strong business lead may be necessary to put the lawyers 'back in their box'. Once the lawyers realise that you really do intend to apologise, they will be of great use in drafting a form of words that delivers a positive PR result while limiting financial liability.

IT staff

Unlike lawyers, the problems of dealing with IT staff are more to do with the nature of their profession than their particular personality traits. Although IT professionals use the phrase *software engineering*, it is important for the manager to understand that it is not an engineering discipline in the same way that civil engineering is. To exhaustively test anything but the simplest of computer programs takes far too much time to be practical. To use mathematics to prove the correctness of anything but the simplest of programs is beyond current technology. The effects of this mathematical 'problem' are well known:

- even the best software programs contain lots of bugs;
- software projects are prone to disastrous cost and time overruns.

There are a number of issues that managers need to be aware of when dealing with IT staff and IT projects, some of which are detailed below.

Software estimating

The first thing to say is that most IT staff are incurable optimists when it comes to estimating how much time and money a piece of software will take to complete. Given the mathematical complexity underlying software, it is not surprising that there are no reliable techniques for software estimating. As a manager you need to know the truth – the only technique that works at all well is by analogy with a past project. Comparing a project with the nearest similar project in size, complexity and functionality can give you a rough idea of time and cost. Even this technique can easily be undermined by the differences between the new project and the project being used for comparison purposes – for example, different staff abilities, or some subtle difference in functionality that proves very hard to implement. If you cannot find a good analogy then your project faces a major risk of time and cost overruns, and even with a good analogy the risks are never small. In summary:

Be afraid, be very afraid.

A few additional, unhelpful hints.

- Any product vendor selling you any technique or tool that makes software development totally predictable is a liar (but the product may be worth buying anyway).
- Quality systems do not solve this problem (but they may be worth using anyway).
- Project management processes cannot solve this problem (but they may highlight the severity of the problem earlier).

Now for a helpful comment.

A third of the way through a software project, the staff on the project will have a very good idea how long the entire project will take – but will still be too optimistic.

This begs the question – how much contingency should the manager add at this stage to get an accurate estimate? The best I can do is offer an observation that I have made, which is that when a software engineer says that the project is 80 per cent complete it is at most only half done. In practice I tend to add about 30 per cent to the estimates I get from staff when they are a third of the way through a project.

Although it is seldom easy, you must plan to review the deadlines and cost estimates about a third of the way through the project. IT staff become demoralised when they know they are working to impossible deadlines.

Software projects usually fail for a few well-known reasons
This following list is very relevant because you as the manager have the responsibility for most of them.

- The requirement for the software was much too ambitious. It is your duty to ensure that the team sticks to the KISS principle – keep it simple, stupid! IT staff tend to love their technology and will seldom question the need for more and more computerisation. This leads to the next problem.

- The requirement for the software becomes divorced from the needs of its ultimate users.

- Weak management! Managers not intervening or making decisions because they do not feel qualified to make judgements about a software project – I will be discussing this in more detail later in the section.

- Continuing acceptance of unrealistic deadlines and unwillingness to brief senior management on the underlying problems.

- Overreliance on consultants.

- Reinventing the wheel, rather than using off-the-shelf packages (and occasionally vice versa).

- Poor handling of the risks posed by suppliers and subcontractors.

- Acceptance of a big-bang introduction of the new software – always run a new system in parallel with any system being replaced. Ensure that there is a fallback mode of operation for when the software falls in a heap – because it will!

Having started this section by saying that software engineering is very different from other engineering disciplines, I look back at this list and see that most of it applies equally to any technical job.

It's the third version of software that works

Most good software engineers know that they need to restructure their software at least twice in the process of developing any substantial piece of code. Usually, they have to hide the fact that they have restructured the software from their managers. Hopefully by explaining this truth to you, you can actively plan for the inevitable rewrites, and gain the respect of your IT staff in the process. Also, if you find that your IT staff do not feel that the software would benefit from restructuring, you need to start worrying about the quality of your IT staff.

Security: a no-win for IT staff

Every profession seems to have its no-win situations, and it is worth understanding them because experts can, understandably, get emotional when you blunder into one. For IT staff, security is one of their major no-win issues. Businesses are very loath to invest in proper IT security, but are quick to shoot the IT experts when security is breached. Please listen carefully when your IT staff discuss security issues.

> listen carefully when your IT staff discuss security issues

Managers' roles in IT projects

Although you may know little or nothing about how to write software, your expertise, judgement and leadership are vital in a number of areas, as follows.

Ensure that the functional specification of the software is appropriate to the needs of your business

It is a well-known fact in the IT industry that many of the problems in software projects stem from mistakes made in the requirements that the software has to meet. I have already mentioned the importance of KISS; you must constantly battle against complexity in the software's functional specification. You must also ensure that the specification of the software meets the requirements of your business – whether the software is for internal use or external sale, the software is a means to an end, not an end in itself. You must also champion the role of the software users, whether they be internal staff within your organisation or your customers' staff. In addition to this role in determining the functional specification, you have an even heavier responsibility in ensuring that the non-functional characteristics of the software meet the needs of your business.

Ensure that the architecture of the software has the properties your business needs

How easy is it to modify the functionality of the software? How easy is it to port the software to a different operating system? How easy is it to interface the software to other pieces of software on the same or different computers? How easy is it for customers to customise the software? How easy is it to scale the software so that it can handle more users or more data? Depending on the purpose of the software, some or all of these may be very good questions – so ask them! It is important for managers to realise that none of the desirable 'ilities' (portability, flexibility, scalability, etc.) will happen by accident; they happen because the software was designed specifically to provide such properties. IT staff tend to be very focused on delivering an initial capability and often give too little attention to how the software will become a long-term part of your business. The way the software is structured (its architecture) will determine the answers to the questions I have posed. You should never need to know about the detailed lines of code within a software system, but you need to ask the right questions to ensure that the architecture is appropriate to your business needs.

Be flexible in adapting business processes to better suit off-the-shelf software

This point appears to rather contradict the previous point. The truth is that many off-the-shelf packages impose severe constraints on the business processes they support. This means that if you want to make the savings from using off-the-shelf software, you have got to be willing to accept the constraints that imposes on your business requirements.

Ensure that appropriate development processes are put in place

What development processes am I thinking about? I am principally talking about the things that IT staff typically know they do badly. The sorts of areas that many IT staff know they are not to be trusted with are:

- testing;
- documentation;
- coding standards;
- code reviews.

And the greatest of these is testing. I strongly advise that you ask early in a project what the test plan is, and ensure that there is adequate time and resources to do it properly. While all competent IT staff will want to test their own code, there is no substitute for energetic, independent software testing.

Managing creative types: how to herd cats

It is easy to parody the personality traits of creative people. Words such as arrogant, petulant, insecure, socially inept, unconventional and prima donna probably spring to mind. Let's look beyond the stereotypes to see what makes creative people tick, and see what management techniques can be successfully deployed on such staff.

The fear of losing the muse

Most creative people do not know 'how they do it'. As a consequence, most creative people worry or, to be more precise, are terrified that their creative ability will desert them. How do you manage this fear in your creative staff? The first thing to do is to create a culture that gives creative people a feeling of security. The best way to show this is by handling creative staff sensitively when their creativity temporarily deserts them. There are some well-proven techniques to deploy.

- Reassure the person that this is a perfectly normal situation.
- Remove deadline pressure.
- Keep the person very busy on routine work – the busier a person is, the more likely they are to regain their creativity.

Creativity often requires obsession

Creativity often requires obsession

Many creative people need to become totally obsessed by a task in order to be creative. If you manage to stop them being obsessive, they will lose their creativity. This means that you need to manage the effects that their obsession causes, but you cannot remove the root cause of the problem. It is important to distinguish the problems that are an inherent part of creativity (which you can do little or nothing about) from those that just happen to be related to creativity (which you can tackle).

The rules don't apply to me

Oh yes they do! This is one of those traits that is related to creativity that you can tackle. I would recommend that you will probably have to be a bit more tolerant of creative staff not sticking to the rules. For example, I have refrained from formally disciplining creative staff when I might have started disciplinary proceedings against a less creative staff member – because obsession does make creative staff more forgetful. However, in the final analysis, there is no reason why creative people should be allowed to get away with not obeying important rules and processes – like filling in their time sheets. A related but subtly different problem concerns individuality.

Creative personalities often do not obey behavioural norms

creative people often stray well outside the norms

In many areas such as dress, behaviour and personal hygiene, creative people often stray well outside the norms expected of staff. As long as the individuality is not offensive to other staff I would recommend that you be as tolerant as your organisation allows. Having to ask a staff member to wash more frequently is definitely one of the more embarrassing tasks that a manager has to face – and you do have to face it.

Lethargy often precedes creativity

Creative staff often suffer from a form of torpor before they embark on a creative task. This is perfectly normal and there is no harm in gently cajoling creative staff to try starting the task.

Creative staff tend to be very sensitive to their work environment

Creative people usually need to achieve an almost trance-like state of concentration, which psychologists refer to as 'flow'. External distractions can easily prevent the attainment of flow. For this reason, creativity and open-plan offices tend to be incompatible. For some creative staff, listening to music on headphones can help. But this is an area where you may need to be creative in your management approach. Working from home or the provision of study rooms may be the answer. Alternatively you may need to reorganise your open-plan accommodation so that those needing quiet are put close together.

brilliant tip

Many creative types are paranoid. Paranoid types need regular desensitising by talking out their irrational fears with them.

Many creative people crave appreciation

It is important to recognise this trait when it is present, or you risk demotivating a creative staff member. It is also important because it provides opportunities for managing creative staff. Sometimes flattery will get you what you want. It can also be possible to sell a job to a creative person by telling them a task has a high profile, and will get them a lot of credit.

Consultants

There is a very narrow dividing line between consultants and some subcontractors. Here my definition of a consultant is someone who gives advice as opposed to someone who rolls their sleeves up and gets their hands dirty doing the real 'work'. I think that this definition points to one of the negative perceptions about consultants. The old saying 'those who can, do, those who can't, teach' is rephrased in many people's minds as 'those who can, do, those who can't, consult'. This is a very sensitive issue with some consultants. My perception is that it tends to be the best consultants who worry about this aspect of their work. One of the very best consultants I have worked with told me the following joke.

Question: What is the definition of a consultant?

Answer: Someone who knows over a hundred ways to make love, but is still a virgin.

It is worth being aware of the potential sensitivity about this issue for consultants, because you mention it to a consultant at your peril.

There are several very strong traits that most consultants share. Understanding these traits can be very useful in helping you manage consultants. In this section I will deal with two different types of interaction you may have with consultants: first, the consultants you or your organisation hire to advise you and, second, the situation where you manage consultants who you hire out to do consultancy for your customers.

Consultants tend to have the mentality of gunslingers
It is important that you do not forget that consultants are hired guns. You can buy their professionalism, but you seldom buy their loyalty. A consequence of this is that consultants you hire need to be very tightly managed. You may manage your own staff in a 'hands-off' manner and because of their loyalty to the team/organisation, and their membership of the team culture, they will not abuse the lack of overt management control. With consultants that you hire, you will do best if you explicitly set the parameters within which they work. If on the other hand your business is selling consultancy, and the consultants work for you, then you need to be aware that the gunslinger mentality does not naturally produce team players, and many consultants are essentially loners who may well put their own interests above the interests of the

> the gunslinger mentality does not naturally produce team players

team. I have found one excellent way to create loyalty in consultants. Most consultants fear that their expertise will get out of date, and that the organisation they work for will milk them for the maximum revenue that their current knowledge can generate, and will then spit them out when their expertise is out of date. If you can offer the consultants in your team the chance to generate new skills, it is much more likely that your consultants will remain loyal to your team.

Consultants tend to be competitive personalities

Much of the training for consultants is very competitive. For example, many management consultants have done MBAs, and many MBA courses are modelled on the highly competitive MBA course structure at Harvard. In addition, many consultancy companies have competitive cultures that are modelled in some way on the culture pioneered by the father of modern consulting companies – McKinsey. It would be too strong to say that all consultants are competitive, but it is a sufficiently marked trait to be worth being aware of. A side-effect of the competitive natures of consultants and consulting firms is that many consultants work very long hours indeed. This means that many consultants work under very high pressure and this can make them somewhat intolerant personalities.

Consultants tend to be very aware of their remuneration

Consultancy is one of the best-paid professions. Unfortunately, combined with competitiveness and weak team-playing skills, this produces many consultants who are very focused on the amount of money they personally earn. There is almost no way a manager of consultants can avoid being sucked into highly aggressive salary negotiations, and few of the techniques that can be applied to staff to moderate their salary aspirations will work. This is one of the main reasons why staff turnover among consultants is so high, and is the main reason why consulting is one of the few professions where the top staff tend to earn salaries similar to what a poacher would pay. One technique that is worth considering is the use of non-monetary rewards. Perks and visible signs of status are often an area where a poacher will not want to match what a consultant already enjoys, for fear of opening the floodgates to dissatisfaction from the poacher's existing consultants, and this can give you a powerful argument for persuading your consultants to stay with you.

Consultants tend to intellectualise rather than empathise

Consultants tend to be analytical personalities who pride themselves on being people who can understand complex problems and who can see how those problems can be solved. Following the advice of a consultant can often cause pain and grief to some of your existing staff. Consultants will often not be very concerned about the pain their advice might cause, and this can cause tensions between consultants and the staff in the organisations they are advising.

The points above address the personal traits and personal behaviours of consultants. The following points look at some characteristics of consultants' professional behaviour.

Beware of consultants telling you what you want to hear

Telling the customer what they want to hear is the oldest trick in the consulting book. The only reason for repeating such a well-known property of consultants is that I see it happening time and time again. The next property of consultancy is almost as well known.

It is better business to tell customers good news than bad news

Just imagine a marketing consultant is brought in to advise on the marketing of a particular product, and finds that the product is almost bound to fail to be profitable. What do you think are the chances that the consultant tells the client that the product is a likely dud? This situation also occurs in many insidious ways with consultants often glossing over fundamental problems that they do not think their customers want to hear about.

Beware of becoming dependent on consultants

It is very easy for one consultancy contract to lead seamlessly into the next. You cannot expect a consultant to tell you that their advice is no longer needed; it is your responsibility to decide when paying for a consultant's advice is no longer cost-effective.

Beware of receiving 'one size fits all' advice

Many consultancy firms seek to maximise their profitability by commoditising their service. They do this by addressing a particular range of problems and training their consultants to pigeonhole the customer's problem into one of a limited number of problem types, each of which has a standard solution. By doing this they can deskill the consultant's job by training their consultants in a standardised method. They can also increase their consultants' productivity by producing reports that contain large amounts of pre-written material. It is your job to ensure that your consultants give advice that is fully relevant to your particular situation. If you are unsure that a consultant could recognise the uniqueness of your situation, it is worth considering dispensing with their services.

Beware of advice based on a flawed method

Another approach to offering a commoditised consultancy service is to offer consultancy based on some trendy structured method. In such a situation, any limitations in the method (and all methods have limitations) can lead to inaccurate advice. The best consultancy comes from the best consultants – if you have bought the services of a well-trained monkey then you only have yourself to blame.

Beware of 'bait and switch'

Given the last two points about how consultancy firms can commoditise their services, it is not surprising that the 'bait and switch' technique is widespread in the consultancy business. This involves using the best consultants to win a contract, and then using second-rate consultants to service the contract.

> the 'bait and switch' technique is widespread in the consultancy business

A word in their defence

Having given consultants a pretty hard time in this section, I would like to say a few words in their defence. There is nothing more depressing than working for a client who has brought in consultants just to justify what they wanted to do anyway. In particular, being brought in to recommend staff cuts has to be one of the most soul-destroying jobs in the world. Working for a client who manages you strongly and genuinely wants insight into their problems is a delight. In short, clients get the consultants they deserve.

Sales people

There are many similarities between the characteristics of sales people and those of consultants. They both tend to be poor team players; they both display a 'hired gun' mentality; they both tend to be motivated by money; they both tend to be very competitive; they both tend to be driven personalities; they both tend to allow integrity to sometimes take a back seat; and they both tend to work very long hours. There is one major difference between consultants and sales people, which is that consultants tend to be highly analytical and rational, whereas sales people tend not to be.

There are a few strong distinguishing characteristics of sales people, as described below.

Sales people are hunters

The really good sales people enjoy chasing their quarry, and delight in the kill. Once they have begun to stalk their prey, they can find it very hard to abandon the hunt. It is important to recognise this quality if you manage sales people because a lot of them will be willing to do unreasonable things to clinch a deal. The sorts of problem that you may encounter are:

- offering too large a discount on the price;

Sales people are hunters

- making unrealistic promises, such as an impossible delivery time;
- offering too many, or impossible, changes to the standard product offering;
- offering too many sweeteners, such as free advice;
- overselling the capabilities of the product.

It is your job as the manager to set the precise parameters under which your sales people operate, and to exercise discipline when (not if) those parameters are breached.

Sales people are not team players

Sales people often do not have a good relationship with product/service delivery staff. Sales people feel, with some justification, that they understand the customer better than the 'back-room boys'; that the value of their views on how the product/service should be developed to make it more saleable are not properly recognised; that they are the 'front line' of the organisation and that everyone else should realise that they are only there to support them; and that everyone else in the organisation fails to display a proper 'can do' attitude.

On the other hand, the staff back at base think, with some justification, that the sales people do not understand the complexity and professionalism needed to deliver a quality product or service; they resent being asked to meet impossible deadlines or compromise the quality of the product or service offering; they resent the fact that sales people do not understand the nature of the product/service and ask for features that are not consistent with the product/service ethos; they think that sales people try to keep them away from the customers; and most irritating of all that they have to work their (expletive deleted) off to earn the sales people their bonuses.

Sales people are quick to blame others
I have no idea why this tends to be the case, but from my observations it is a very marked behavioural trait in sales people.

Most sales people expect to work in a bonus culture
If you are a manager who thinks that bonuses are a very crude way to motivate staff, and who uses bonuses sparingly as a motivational aid, you need to be aware of the fact that bonuses are the norm for motivating sales people. As always it is essential to set the parameters of bonuses very carefully.

brilliant example

If a sales bonus is completely based on volume of business then sales people will not be motivated to push for the highest possible price; consequently, it is usually necessary to base bonuses on margins as well as volume.

Managing support staff

The reason I am including this section is because many managers find it difficult to manage staff whose educational and professional backgrounds are often very different from their own. If, like me, you find this difficult, I can offer the following advice:

Lack of academic qualifications does not imply a lack of common sense.

I sometimes think that the most qualified people are often the most lacking in common sense. Common sense and enthusiasm are two key qualities to look for in support staff.

It is reasonable to insist that support staff offer a very reliable service

The key to good support is its reliability. It is not acceptable if your team members feel that they have to constantly check up on support staff, rather than trusting them to get on with it.

You may need to train your team how to get the best out of support staff

Do not expect that your team members will naturally know how to use support staff to best effect. Some common misconceptions are:

- all support staff are idiots;
- all support staff are as knowledgeable as the people they support;
- all support staff are mind-readers;
- all support staff are too busy to help me;
- my job is the most urgent one.

The knack is knowing how much detail and background information you need to give a particular support person, and whether it needs to be written down or can be given verbally.

Some support staff can work with a less than precise specification of a task, while others will need a fair amount of detail spelling out. It is also important to let the support staff know the deadlines for the work, and how the work relates to their other priorities.

Investing in training support staff can pay great dividends
Many support staff have never been told how to give good customer service. For example, many support staff have never been told the importance of giving the people they support feedback on the progress of a task and warning them in good time of any likely delays. In addition, the increasing use of computing technology in the workplace means you will have to invest in keeping support staff's skills up to date.

> invest in keeping support staff's skills up to date

Insist that support staff be treated with respect
Some people will treat support staff like servants, without consideration or courtesy. Make sure that you let the team know that such behaviour is unacceptable. I went so far as to order the support staff to report the names of discourteous staff to me; I then made it clear to the rude staff that unless they mended their ways they would have support withdrawn from them. Politeness does not, however, mean that the team should tolerate sloppy service. If support is not totally reliable then support staff should be politely, but firmly, made aware that they have let a team member down.

Summary

You must understand what your experts are telling you. Insist that issues be explained to you in a way that you can understand. Keep asking questions until you do understand.

Beware of experts who:

- advocate particular solutions;
- say that something is impossible;
- seek to make you dependent on their continued advice.

When dealing with lawyers, remember that they tend to be risk-averse, hate moving quickly and like a good argument (preferably in court).

When dealing with IT staff, remember that software is not like traditional engineering disciplines. Estimating software projects is a black art, largely based on comparison with past projects, although one useful technique is to redo your estimates about a third of the way through the project.

Most software projects fail for reasons that are within management's control:

- inadequate requirements;
- poor consideration of the users' view of the software;
- too much complexity in the software's specification;
- unrealistic deadlines;
- management's failure to confront problems because they feel they are not qualified to intervene.

You have other key roles in managing software projects:

- ensuring that the non-functional properties of the software are addressed by the system architecture;
- ensuring that there are adequate processes for testing, code

management, documentation, coding standards and code reviews.

When dealing with creative types, you must remember that many of them fear the loss of their creativity and will need continuous reassurance. Creative people often have to be obsessive in order to be creative, and you will need to decide how tolerant you will be of their obsessions, and other unattractive behavioural traits.

Consultants tend to have a gunslinger mentality. Many will not be team players. They will often be very self-centred and focused on money.

Sales people have many of the same characteristics as consultants. You need to remember that they are hunters. They will usually demand financial bonuses and will react very crudely to any financial incentives you set – so set them very carefully.

You should insist that support staff give highly reliable service. Any lack of qualifications does not imply a lack of common sense. You may well need to train your team in how to get the best out of their support staff.

CHAPTER 6

Organising
your team

Organising yourself

The principles of time management are well known to most of us and, if not, there are many good books on the subject. However well the techniques of good time management work for you, I would give the following words of warning:

No matter how well you manage your time, you cannot do everything you want to do.

This means that you must employ techniques to actually reduce the number of tasks that you do, such as:

- delegation;
- dropping low-priority tasks.

brilliant timesaver

Reduce your level of perfectionism on appropriate tasks. I have seen a number of managers work themselves into the ground because they had no notion of doing a job *well enough*. Put bluntly, a lot of the work you will spend your time doing is not vitally important to the future of the team. You need to discipline yourself to identify work that can be done less well and then ruthlessly limit the amount of time you put into such tasks.

Before looking at team organisation I will say a few words on the second item on the list above.

Dropping low-priority tasks

I once conducted an experiment: I was getting buried by the volume of emails from other parts of my organisation demanding answers of various kinds. I ignored them all and waited to see how many people chased me. Approximately 90 per cent never chased me. Of the remaining 10 per cent I replied as briefly as possible to about 80 per cent and then dealt diligently with the remaining 20 per cent I thought important. Result: I dealt with about 2 per cent diligently.

For fear of incriminating myself further I will not go on to describe other experiments I conducted into which jobs I found that I could ignore without getting into trouble. I am not recommending that you copy my somewhat irresponsible behaviour; the reason for describing these experiments is that I would suggest you think carefully about your priorities and consider whether some of your lower-priority jobs can be left undone so that you can give more time to the really important jobs.

> some of your lower-priority jobs can be left undone

One aspect of identifying which tasks cannot be dropped safely is to be aware of which tasks your boss is particularly interested in. Being brutally cynical, it is worth finding out which of the tasks you do could impact on your boss' bonus, because you drop those at your peril!

Management tasks

Before looking at possible ways of organising your team it is worth reviewing a typical list of the major tasks the average manager has to do:

- firefighting – people queuing up to ask for your help in resolving problems;
- business strategy formulation;
- staff management issues (such as staff appraisals and pay setting);
- staff and other resource allocation;
- operations management (finance, accommodation and all the other niff, naff and trivia of running a team);
- interfacing with the rest of the organisation (both routine and special initiatives);
- head of state (someone needs to wheel the boss out);
- emissary (setting up links to other groups inside and outside the organisation);
- sales person;
- negotiator;
- schmoozing with customers;
- reviewing the outputs of the team.

Controlling the team's finances

To manage your team effectively you have to organise and control the finances of your team. There are plenty of training courses on the basics of finance and it is likely that your organisation can recommend an appropriate one. Likewise there are plenty of books, and many very useful resources available on the Internet. You need to understand the concepts that underlie the 'balance sheet' for your team's activities. Not understanding the financial status of your team is like flying a fast jet, in fog, at low level, in the mountains, without instruments – potentially fatal. Personally I find this aspect of a manager's job incredibly boring, but if asked if I mind doing it I would answer 'not when you consider the alternative'.

Can you just rely on your organisation's financial systems? In a word … no. There are several reasons.

- There is a computing term called GIGO – garbage in, garbage out. One reason for keeping your own books is to spot the mistakes in the official figures.

- You often need much simpler figures to control your team's operations, and in the company's systems it will often be difficult to see the wood from the trees.

- You will often need to drill-down into a particular part of the figures to understand what appears to be an anomaly. Corporate systems are often very poor at drill-down.

- The organisation's systems are structured to control the financial aspects that are key to the organisation, for example control of cash flow. Often you will share an interest in those aspects, but will almost certainly have other requirements that your organisation's systems do not support.

Taking the last point a bit further, using the fast jet analogy again – what instruments do you need? Do you need speed and height? What else do you need? Work out what aspects of the finances are really key to your team's financial health and then set up your spreadsheets to monitor those aspects. It may be current and future utilisation of staff; it may be the flow of incoming orders; it may be spend with subcontractors; it may be cash flows and invoicing.

There are a few tips I can offer.

- Remember GIGO applies to your figures too. Try to cross-check your figures for internal consistency, consistency with reality (200 per cent utilisation is unusual), and consistency with your organisation's figures.

- Don't blindly trust your spreadsheets. They are only as good as the formulae in them. It is easy to mistype formulae or to write a formula that is plausible but wrong (if tax is 15 per cent then a without-tax price is not 15 per cent less than the with-tax price). It is always worth getting someone experienced to check your spreadsheet design.

- If you are inexperienced then ask someone experienced what the classic pitfalls are (exclusive of tax versus inclusive of tax; forgetting that everyone takes leave in the summer; not making a realistic allowance for how long invoices take to raise and be processed; etc.).

- Don't forget that the measure of a good set of spreadsheets is that they alert you to problems in good time. This means that you will need to be projecting your key financial indicators into the future. In order for this to work, you have to keep the data in your spreadsheets up to date.

Delegating responsibilities

What to delegate

The first thing to stress is that the organisation of your team has to be built around the skills of the staff you have or the staff you can recruit. The approach of designing an idealised team structure, and then trying to fill all the posts within that structure, can only work if the team is large enough so that you are likely to find enough staff with the requisite skills. Given that this book is aimed at the lowest level of managers in an organisation, you will do much better to build a team structure around the people you have to hand.

You need to focus on the fact that you will only have a limited number of staff who can lead a project or task and be relied on to bring it in successfully. Say you have five such staff, then you can only do five things really well – so make sure those five staff are working on the five most important roles. You will then have to manage the fact that other tasks are quite likely not to run smoothly.

The obvious role you can delegate is operations management. The type of personality that makes for a good leader is frequently not the right person to handle the day-to-day detailed operations of the team. You can delegate operations management at a number of levels. At one extreme you can pass off most of the responsibilities to a professional business administrator. At the other extreme you can retain the major responsibilities and have a reliable office assistant to execute the bulk of the routine duties (possibly part time).

you can delegate operations management at a number of levels

If you are delegating some of your responsibilities you will want to consider having a group of trusted lieutenants who act as a small board with yourself as chairperson/chief executive. If you have the right people, who get on well together, this can work wonderfully. However, if there is no group with the right chemistry then it is better to act alone as the leader figure.

You will probably be required to nominate a deputy or deputies. There are two distinct ways of handling this. The deputy can be used solely to deputise in your absence, with the expectation that they will try not to make major decisions in your absence. The other way is to have your deputy empowered at all times and you ensure they are kept in the picture so that they can make real decisions. Which method you choose will depend on how much you trust, and how well you can work with, your deputy.

If you have appropriate staff it can be useful to have members of the team working directly for you, even if only for part of their time. Such staff could act as general assistants to you or they could do particular projects on your behalf, such as implementing one of the initiatives dreamed up by head office. This approach has three beneficial effects: first, it will reduce the load on you; second, it can be useful for developing the careers of the staff who work for you; and, last, the staff who work directly for you can help you understand what issues the members of the team are worrying about.

Depending on the size of your team you may need to introduce a level of management between yourself and the rest of the team. If you have to do this you are moving away from the type of manager this book is particularly targeted at. There is, however, a limit to the size of team you can manage in a totally flat hierarchy.

One area that is worthy of careful thought is the level of administrative support you put into your team. One extreme position is to hire more value-creating staff and make them do their own photocopying, travel arrangements and the like. The other extreme view is that it is crazy to have highly paid staff doing menial tasks. My own view is that excellent support is very cost-effective, but poor support is worse than useless.

How to delegate

What are the issues that make effective delegation so hard? In the introductory chapter to this book, I included a literal reading warning which warned the reader to interpret any advice I give in the unique context that the reader works within. Delegation is a classic example where the manager must understand the context in which responsibility is being passed to someone in their team.

Defining exactly what responsibilities and authorities you have delegated

This can be really difficult to do, but if delegation is to work then you will have to invest significant thought and time in defining as precisely as possible what responsibilities and authorities you are delegating. It is inevitable that you will have to refine those definitions as you go along, and this implies that you need to have a good working relationship with the person doing the delegated role/task.

How much can you trust the person you are delegating to?

You really have got to address this issue. All too often you will be in a position where you either do not know if you trust the person, because they have little or no track record that you are aware of, or you have reasons to distrust the person.

If you do not know if you can trust the person then you will need to consider two issues very carefully – deciding on the right level of visibility and control, and can you afford for the person to fail and what do you do if they fail? You should also consider what level of support an inexperienced person, tackling a new responsibility for the first time, needs. If appropriate, you may wish to coach/mentor the person.

> decide on the right level of visibility

If you have reason to distrust the person you are considering delegating to, then you may have a real problem. You will want to increase visibility and control, and also do more contingency planning in case they fail. It is easy to reach the limiting case where it would be more cost-effective not to delegate. You also need to ask yourself if there is anything that the person could do to increase your trust in them, and then ask yourself why you have not done anything about it.

Deciding on the right level of visibility and control

Many managers believe the common fallacy that delegation is a black and white issue, and that there is no point in delegating to someone if you are going to have to monitor them. In my view you should maintain a level of visibility appropriate to their experience, track record and the level of damage that would be done by them failing. It is worth discussing with the person you are delegating to what level of visibility and control you will be exercising. This is far better than the not uncommon scenario of setting someone off and then panicking when something goes wrong, and either taking the responsibility off them or putting draconian controls in place.

Can I afford for the person to fail, and what do I do if they fail?

You need to ask and answer this question. If the answer is that failure will inflict major damage, then you may well want to raise this issue with the person involved before they start and openly discuss with them what your plans are if the person hits major problems.

You must allow people to do jobs differently from the way you would do them

You have to school yourself not to interfere if someone does a task very differently from the way you would have done it. If you see problems with the way they are doing a job, then you may wish to alert them to the possible dangers, but if they are responsible then they must make the final choice of how to do the job.

You must not undermine people with delegated authority.

You can undermine people who you have delegated authority to in a host of subtle ways.

- By attending meetings at which they should be taking the lead – if you are there, people at the meeting will naturally look to you for decisions.

- By not giving them all the information they need to do their jobs properly, for example the context in which they are working.

- By not stopping people more senior than them interfering.

- By not making it clear that you will accept full responsibility if things go wrong.

- By not making it obvious that they can come to you for advice and support.

- By criticising them in public.

- By making decisions that either they should take, or which they should be consulted about.

- By putting in excessive visibility and controls.

- By putting in inadequate visibility and controls.
- By taking an interest in unnecessary details.
- By belittling the task or role they are doing.
- By meddling – for example, by discussing inappropriate issues with people who work for them.
- By changing the ground rules frequently.

You must define success and failure criteria
People need to know if they are doing the task/role in a way that you are happy with. If you cannot give well-defined success and failure criteria, then you will need to give regular informal feedback on how well they are doing.

Try to avoid delegation in response to a crisis
I often see managers only delegating tasks when they become heavily overloaded. I hope I have made it clear that delegating a task needs a considerable amount of care and preparation – exactly the sorts of things you will not do if you are under considerable pressure. It is much better to have delegated responsibilities in time to avoid becoming overloaded. If you have to delegate in response to an urgent situation then you need to take the time to do it properly – and if you choose to rush it, don't come whining to me when it all goes wrong!

Using consultants

We have all seen organisations that become overly dependent on management consultants. There are, however, times when hiring someone from outside your team is appropriate.

- When an outside viewpoint is needed. You and your team may well be basing your decisions on implicit assumptions that an outsider can challenge. Outsiders will also be dispassionate, which can help counteract the passion in yourself and the team.

- When you want to bring in a particular skill on a temporary basis. For example, if you are trying to build a new business opportunity in a market area that is new to your team, it can be useful to hire marketing and sales consultants with experience in the new market area, until it is clear whether that opportunity is, or is not, going to be successful.

Summary

The way you delegate responsibilities is one of the principal techniques you can use to control your workload. It is also a way of covering for areas that you are weak in.

There is no single right way to organise your team. This chapter gives a range of techniques that can be used *if, and only if, you have the right staff available in your team to delegate the responsibilities to* – you have to work with the staff you have available.

CHAPTER 7

Brilliant
business tips

Introduction

Your business acumen can make or break your team. You can have all the best people skills in the world, but if you can't deliver your financial bottom line then the show may well be over. Continually honing your business skills should be a top priority and, for this reason, I want to devote a whole chapter to this. Really I need a whole book to adequately cover the business skills a front-line manager needs, but by looking at four core business activities and pulling out the most important brilliant tips in each, I can give you a very good head start. There are lots of good books on more specific business skills such as negotiations, selling, finances, presentations and the like, so I will stick to four broad areas:

1 developing products and services;
2 marketing;
3 pitching;
4 business processes.

And finish the chapter with some important miscellaneous tips.

Products and services

Don't believe anyone who says that marketing is more important than your products and services. In fact, don't believe anything is more important than a brilliant product or service. A brilliant product isn't a guarantee of success, but nothing (and I do mean nothing) does more to ensure the success of your business.

---

brilliant tip

Manage your passion

Having a great idea and then building it into a profitable business isn't rocket science, so why does it so often go wrong? In a word the biggest danger is also the key to your success – *passion*. It is easy to see why most businesses are founded on passion. Passion provides the commitment, energy, enthusiasm and determination to drive through the inevitable setbacks to ultimate success. Passion is so important that many organisations will not pursue a new business opportunity without a passionate leader to champion the product.

The following tips will help you manage the downside of passion – it can so easily blind you to the reality of a situation.

---

brilliant tip

Wherever possible, be a cheapskate

Never be tempted to show your commitment by investing lots of money. However convinced you are of your ultimate success, you must spend money as if failure is the most likely outcome. Keeping your costs under the tightest control has a double benefit: it makes it easier to show a profit, and it also reduces the damage if you have to abandon the business opportunity. It is usually better to try a number of thrifty opportunities than risk everything on a big, expensive gamble. Remember that Pareto's 80:20 law means that you can usually achieve a professional-looking job with only a fraction of the expenditure that a gold-plated solution would cost (you can get 80 per cent of the effect for 20 per cent of the cost).

A related tip.

brilliant tip

Don't try to run until you have shown you can walk

Try to minimise your investment until it is clear that the business is breaking out of the 'early adopter' type of customer. The moment you find you can easily increase your customer base is the time to put the pedal to the metal.

A second reason for going reasonably slowly to start with can be summed up in the following tip.

brilliant tip

Don't be afraid to change your business proposition

One of the best things about passion is that it leads to activity, and activity often leads to insight ... so don't be afraid to use that insight. As you talk to potential customers, and get genuine feedback about your proposition, you will often stumble across a much better product or service to sell.

To help implement this tip you need to make sure you can incorporate changes ...

brilliant tip

Design your product or service to be flexible and adaptable

One of the few areas I suggest you invest more than the bare minimum in is engineering your product or service so that it can easily be adapted as you find out what the customers really want to buy. A bit of investment upfront in making it easy to adapt your product or service is nearly always money well spent.

Of course the ultimate form of change is death ...

brilliant tip

You must be ready and willing to pull the plug

There is absolutely no shame in admitting that a business proposition is an honourable failure. The problem is that your passion will be whispering in your ear that one last push will see you through to success. How do you ignore that insidious whisper? You need to set clear goals and targets so that you know when the time has come to pull the plug.

I would also advise that you adopt the following tip.

brilliant tip

Get access to authoritative, dispassionate advice

The best possible situation is if your boss is keeping a close eye on you and can tell you when to pull the plug. Failing that, you need access to dispassionate advisers you trust.

This leads neatly on to the next set of tips, which focus on the need to consider your proposition dispassionately.

brilliant tip

Ensure the 'buy it' proposition is truly compelling

I will illustrate this point with a mortifying example from my own history. I was in charge of a business that was selling a technology that made it much easier to create a piece of software that could be easily ported to all the different variants of the UNIX operating system. The technology was unique, very clever and slashed porting costs by more than half. We knew that companies that were selling their software products on many UNIX systems often spent as much as 50 per cent of their R&D budgets just doing the porting exercise. Surely this was a compelling proposition? Oh no it wasn't! The problem was that porting was perceived as a low-risk activity, you just threw money at it and it was solved. Management were not prepared to invest their time changing something that worked just to save money, they were only willing to invest their efforts in solving something that was causing them pain.

Some useful points to consider in identifying a truly compelling 'buy it' proposition.

- Does it solve one of the customer's top three problems? Like aspirin it is very easy to sell something that makes a nasty pain go away.

- How easy is the product to own after you buy it? If your product or service requires a significant effort on the part of the customer to use it then your proposition becomes a lot less compelling. This can even be as simple as the fact that publishers find it easier to sell a short book than a long book.

- If there is an existing market for your product or service, are you clearly differentiated from the competition? If you are not well differentiated you will need other major advantages, such as a strong existing brand you can exploit or much better channels to market.

● Do you have a really simple, clear, persuasive 'elevator pitch' – can you tell a customer what your proposition is in less than a minute?

● Has some change in the world made your product or service a 'must buy'? A good example is if it helps handle some new law or regulation that has been introduced.

brilliant tip

Check your proposition is defensible

One of the common myths of business is that being first to market is really important. It is the first organisation to create a major brand that usually grabs the spoils. Time and again a 'fast follower' grabs the market from the 'prime mover'. If you are the prime mover (first to market), how do you stop a competitor (the fast follower) with better brands, financing and channels from creating a competitive product and taking your market away from you?

This leads to the obvious next step.

brilliant tip

Use any protection available to you

This can be any mixture of patents, copyright, trade secrets, know-how, non-disclosure agreements, registered trademarks, brand names, exclusive contracts with distributors, etc.

brilliant tip

Work out how you will scale your product or service if business increases

Handling 100 customers is very different from handling 10; 1000 customers are very different from 100; and so on. Likewise handling a £1,000,000 contract is very different from a £100,000 one. For example, if you are selling a service that depends on a limited supply of skilled staff you are going to find scaling very hard. Have you got, or can you develop, the business processes to cope as the order of magnitude of customers (or contract size) keeps increasing? If you are selling direct can you get more sales people or find indirect channels quickly? Are you going to need to find investment fast as the business suddenly takes off (and businesses tend to grow in sharp spurts)?

brilliant tip

Work out what is the maximum amount of money you could lose

Developing a new business proposition is a risk; this tip helps you realise how big a risk. Can you/your organisation afford to lose this much money? If not then don't pursue it. Can your career survive losing this much money? Is there any way you can limit your losses? Use this figure to guide any future decision to pull the plug on a failing business opportunity … like all professional gamblers, try to never exceed your initial estimate of the maximum you are willing to lose. Wherever possible try to avoid pursuing an opportunity where the downside of failure is great; or putting it another way, always give priority to those opportunities where the downside of failure is small.

I am certainly not going to waste your time telling you how to do a discounted cash flow calculation, but I have one further financial tip for working out whether to pursue an opportunity.

brilliant tip

Work out how much you have to sell to break even

If the amount you have to sell to break even is at all scary then I suggest you search for a different opportunity to pursue! As I have mentioned before this is a very good reason to be a skinflint – the lower your costs the easier it is to break even. Once you are breaking even then your investment to that point will be viewed by your bosses as sunk costs, so they are likely to let you keep trying to break through to better sales.

Given the eternal truth that almost all businesses fall behind their initial sales projections, getting to break even as soon as possible is a very important issue for you.

That is all the financial tips I feel it is worth highlighting: I am sure you will have all the other bases covered. This leaves me one last tip on proposition analysis that highlights an area that I see people (including myself in the past) falling into time and again.

brilliant tip

For goodness sake, validate your proposition

If I had a pound for every business opportunity I have seen start without having talked to a single prospective customer, I would be a rich man. The key validation you should always do includes:

- writing down your elevator pitch;
- trying your proposition out on prospective customers;
- trying your proposition out on the people who will have to sell it – in particular, show your elevator pitch to them;
- trying your proposition out on experienced people you trust;
- studying your competitors properly. No ... I said properly!
- if possible producing a prototype of your product/service to show people.

brilliant tip

Wherever possible fly below the radar

My personal advice is to keep as low a profile as possible for your business proposition. If, for example, there is a limit above which you have to make a special case for investment funding, then try to keep below that limit. Being a bit Machiavellian, it is better to estimate investment costs a bit low and then if they go over the limit for which you should have sought high-level approval, you will probably get away with it. If your business proposition has a high profile you may well attract the sort of 'help' from head office that you would much rather do without.

There are however sources of help you should seek out ...

brilliant tip

Use good sources of free support within your organisation

Many organisations fund a significant infrastructure from central resources that are available at no direct charge to you when launching and growing a new product or service. These can include:

- PR and market research;
- legal and contracts support;
- marketing support, such as advice on brands, trademarks, etc.;
- advice on, and sometimes design, and even production of, marketing material;
- review of business plans;
- sales – both explicit sales teams, and also through less direct sources of sales leads such as account managers and the like.

Take care not to get caught in the radar beam, but using these resources can save you so much money that it is worth the risk.

Speaking of risks the next tip could save your career.

brilliant tip

Never publicly embarrass your organisation

It is vital that you consider if there is any significant risk that you could end up getting bad publicity, being sued, or even worse in court, for example, for a breach of health and safety regulations. Any significant risks make a new business proposition much less attractive. If, in spite of these risks, you decide to proceed, you must ignore my tip about staying below the radar because you need to raise these risks with your marketing and legal experts in order to understand how to mitigate them in the best ways possible.

brilliant tip

Remember to be a fast follower if you have the appropriate assets

Most people like to think of themselves as the innovator who is a prime mover. If you work for a company with strong relevant assets, such as:

- an existing brand you can leverage;
- good sales force and/or channels to market;
- scaleable processes and/or infrastructure – e.g. manufacturing capability;
- money to out-market the prime mover;

then being a fast follower can be the easiest possible route to making a lot of money with only a modest amount of risk – the prime mover has taken the risks to create the market and you may be able to walk in and reap the rewards. Don't let your pride lead you to miss such opportunities.

Marketing

Although there are some good marketing books in the section on *Suggested reading* at the end of this chapter I thought it worth giving a few basic tips.

brilliant tip

Marketing messages must be very simple

Customers' perceptions of your products and services and your brands will be very simplistic and can usually be expressed in a few simple words or phrases. One of the commonest mistakes is to make your marketing message too complex. As an example, Volvo built their brand based on a single word – *safety*.

brilliant tip

Repeat marketing messages *ad nauseam*

Just because you get fed up with repeating a marketing message time after time, doesn't mean your audience will get sick of it. A consistent, simple, constantly repeated message is essential.

brilliant tip

Names matter

You may well not be in the business of registering your brand names, but you should certainly use distinctive, memorable names that do not infringe anyone else's trademarks. It is well worth checking that the .com domain name based on the brand name is still free. A good name is the single best start to building brand awareness.

brilliant tip

Build your marketing on benefits not features

Emphasising features rather than benefits is a very common mistake indeed. Some features are closely related to benefits – for example, a car engine with 16 valves is likely be more powerful than an engine of the same capacity with 8 valves – but it is best to find out what your customers value and base your marketing messages on these benefits. For example, the Japanese success in car manufacture was largely based on satisfying customers' desire for highly reliable vehicles.

brilliant tip

Niche marketing is often a great strategy

There is a natural tendency to make your offerings appeal to as wide an audience as possible. Paradoxically, you are often better marketing an offering to a tightly defined market niche. The more precisely your product fits your target customers' needs the easier it will be to sell, and the easier your market will be to defend.

brilliant tip

Don't be afraid to be bold

Given the barrage of different marketing messages being aimed at your customers, you will want to make your message distinctive. A 'me-too' message will probably get lost in the noise.

brilliant tip

PR is often cheaper and better than advertising

When someone mentions a marketing campaign, many people immediately think of advertising. Mass media advertising is high cost and low impact and should be left to supporting the vendors of global brands. Highly targeted advertisements, such as sponsored links on search engines, can be an entirely different proposition. For raising brand awareness the cheap and effective option is to use PR to place articles in the mass media and specialist press.

Pitching

Business books tend to delight in proposing quick-fix solutions that will transform your career. This section is the nearest I have ever come to writing such material. There is little that helps your career more than winning – getting that job you have applied for; winning that contract you have bid for; presenting a pitch that impresses the hell out of a customer; etc. The reason that this section is so important is that I will describe a precise list of dos and don'ts that work really well ... and which so few people seem to follow. If you choose to follow them then it should do your career a lot of good.

brilliant tip

Do your revision/research

Very few people would sit an examination having done no revision, but once out of the academic environment many people throw away that discipline. Would you go to a job interview without researching the organisation's website? Unbelievably I have interviewed quite a few candidates fresh from college who either have done no research, or done only very cursory research. If you are trying to win a contract do you know as much as you possibly can about the customer organisation? Have you used any inside information within your organisation to find out about the people you are dealing with? Do you know the background against which the invitation to tender has emerged? Have you tried asking questions to gain extra information from the person/organisation you are pitching to?

As an author I submitted my first book to a publisher who I later found out didn't publish many books similar to the one that I had written. A single visit to a large bookshop would have shown me that I had chosen the wrong publisher – inexcusable incompetence … but so common.

The Internet provides a wonderful medium for many of your research needs but you need to back it up with more old fashioned media when appropriate and also with intelligence from your network of contacts and any other people you can find who have relevant information.

An important revision technique is the basis of the next tip.

brilliant tip

Spot, and prepare for, likely questions

I can illustrate the efficacy of this technique with an anecdote from my own experience. When I first joined my company it was part of the UK Scientific Civil Service and promotions were awarded on the recommendation of a promotion board. The boards comprised three people – an administrator as chairman and two senior scientists/ engineers who were quite likely to be experts in specialities that were different from the candidate's. The candidate gave a 5-minute presentation of their work over the past 3 years and then the board members asked general and technical questions for 40 minutes. Over the years I must have prepared over 30 people for their boards. Spotting likely questions and preparing the key points to be made in answer to them was the single most important part of the preparation. Typically a candidate was able to spot approximately 80 per cent (yes, 80 per cent!) of the questions they were actually asked, which gave them a tremendous advantage in the boards.

It is easy to see why this technique is so successful.

● It makes you put yourself in the position of the person being pitched to. As a consequence you get inside their head and think about your offering from their perspective.

● It makes you crystallise your offering so that you can articulate the key benefits you offer and the key differentiators from your competitors.

● It makes you think about the weaknesses of your offering and gets you thinking how you can best mitigate these weaknesses, or, even better, how you can present them as strengths.

● It allows you to give a polished performance in a question and answer session, which is an important part of many pitches.

The last point regarding question and answer sessions highlights the importance of the next tip.

brilliant tip

Rehearse – for real and in your head

All important pitches should be run through at least one dress rehearsal. Major issues such as the clarity of the pitch, and the tone of the pitch (arrogant, aggressive, defensive, apologetic) will be ruthlessly exposed in a dress rehearsal … for goodness sake don't expose these mistakes to the intended recipients of your pitch. Many more minor, but still very important, problems can also be ironed out, such as getting your timings spot on. Make sure that the people reviewing the pitch have seen any documentation that is relevant, e.g. instructions supplied to bidders, so that they can check that the pitch is compliant with any rules that have been laid down.

You can also run the pitch through repeatedly in your head, which will help you fix the key issues in your mind and will help expose questions that might arise.

If the pitch is written rather than being presented in person, then the equivalent tip is this one.

brilliant tip

Get a written pitch reviewed

The arguments are the same as for having a dress rehearsal, with some obvious analogies – comments on written style will replace presentation style, etc. It is important to ensure that at least one review is openly acknowledged to be combative, with the reviewer ruthlessly trying to pull the pitch apart.

I mentioned previously the need for reviewers to check that a pitch is compliant with any rules that are laid down. This is at the centre of the next tip.

brilliant tip

Read the question and do what you are told to do

Every school and university teaches this basic piece of examination technique, but I have seen many pitches where the person/organisation being pitched to has said what they want, and what they do not want, in a pitch, and they then receive a non-compliant pitch. There is no excuse for this mistake. You may courageously decide to pitch non-compliantly because you feel that is your best chance of winning, but don't do it by mistake.

Create a compelling elevator pitch

An elevator pitch is based on the idea that you get into a lift and find yourself standing beside someone you would like to pitch to. What can you say to your captive audience in the minute or so ride between floors that makes a totally compelling pitch for your offering. The idea of an elevator pitch is a brilliant technique for making you focus on the key benefits your offering delivers.

A possibly apocryphal example that demonstrates the perfect elevator pitch is one for Ridley Scott's film *Alien – Jaws* in space. Whilst you will seldom achieve such simple perfection, you need to create the shortest, punchiest elevator pitch you possibly can. A useful technique is to create a range of elevator pitches of different lengths, e.g. one sentence, one paragraph, and one page.

The next tip expands on the elevator pitch.

Identify your win themes and key selling points

It is worth remembering in pitching that your selling points don't have to be unique selling points. Your win themes may be incredibly mundane. For example having a win theme of being the cheapest compliant bid isn't very sexy, but it can, in the right situation, be a winning theme. Whatever you are pitching for you must clearly focus on the parts of your pitch that you think are going to win for you, and these parts need to be appropriately emphasised in your pitch.

brilliant tip

Avoid the obvious presentational errors

The following list of common pitfalls is pretty obvious but warrants a quick reminder.

- Don't be long-winded.
- Always tell the truth – being caught out in a lie, or being economical with the truth, is a very serious mistake.
- Never, ever talk over the customer (yes I have seen this done quite frequently!).
- Dress appropriately – if in doubt, err on the smart side.
- If pitching to an audience that contains people who are not native English speakers then avoid talking fast, using colloquialisms or using humour.
- Get the administrative details spot on – take your own projector, take a back-up of your presentation on a USB stick, remember the hand-outs, remember to provide decent refreshments when you are the host, run to time, and for goodness sake don't turn up late!

brilliant tip

Be enthusiastic

One of the sure-fire ways to create a likeable persona is to project enthusiasm. Enthusiastic people are very easy to like and engage with. You do however need to be careful not to forget to listen carefully to the customer – don't be in output mode all the time. It is really important to engage in a true conversation, and to ask intelligent questions.

Business processes

The processes by which you manage your finances, staff, customers, product development, maintenance and support will have a significant effect on your efficiency (and hence costs), quality, and risks. These are all potentially good things, but there is a potential downside to your processes that the next tip highlights.

brilliant tip

Don't let your processes ruin your agility

There is a natural tendency when a mistake happens to add something extra to your processes to stop it happening again. As a consequence your processes will tend to become more complex and cumbersome over time. Eventually your processes may get to the state where nothing can happen quickly. An alternative strategy is to accept that mistakes will happen, and to maintain sufficient visibility to spot mistakes early, and retain enough agility to address those mistakes quickly.

brilliant tip

Carefully select your control measures

In management-speak this is the tight aspect of a *loose/tight system*. It is usually best to select only a few aspects of your business you keep very tight control over. Possible examples are running costs, project reviews and capital expenditure. There is no magic recipe here; you need to select controls that suit your business, your own organisation's controls, the culture … in short, everything. You need to be aware of the fact that your staff will respond very literally to the tight processes, which can cause unforeseen and undesirable consequences. As an example, you need to set bonuses and incentives very carefully, otherwise they may have unfortunate, distorting effects on staff behaviour.

brilliant tip

Ensure your team's outputs are properly reviewed

Reviews are one of the best ways of maintaining high-quality outputs. Ensuring that written outputs, software code, designs, etc. are reviewed by qualified staff is one of the best ways of ensuring that mistakes do not escape outside your team. You may want to take a prominent personal role in reviewing as a means of showing your commitment to quality, and giving you visibility of your team's outputs.

brilliant tip

Top-down processes only work for well-defined tasks

A top-down process requires that a task be planned in detail before it is undertaken. A bottom-up process does a bit of the task and then uses what has been found out to help plan the next part of the task. Top-down tends to work best when you are doing a well-understood task. Bottom-up is much more suitable when you are attempting something for the first time. Managers tend to feel much more comfortable with the predictability of top-down processes, but using them for poorly defined tasks is futile.

brilliant tip

Processes often break down as a team grows in size

There tend to be natural discontinuities relating to team size. A team of, say, five people can rely largely on informal processes because everyone knows what everyone else is doing. A team of up to, say, 20–30 people can work without intermediate levels of management, with you knowing everyone and everything that is going on. Much bigger than 20–30 and you will have to structure the team so that you do not have such direct control over all the activities of the team. If your team is growing, be alert for signs that your organisational structure and processes are no longer able to cope, and redesign them.

Discontinuities in team size often coincide with other business discontinuities. For example, if one of your products or services has suddenly broken through into the mainstream market you will often have to cope with major business issues, as well as a sudden growth in the size of your team. Many small companies fail to manage such discontinuities successfully. If you work within a larger organisation there should be a support structure to help your team through periods of rapid growth. In such situations designing and staffing a management structure suitable for your new size and new business opportunities should be your top priority; otherwise you and your team will run faster and faster and faster, and it is almost inevitable that the team will 'lose the plot'.

Miscellaneous tips

brilliant tip

Use the 80:20 rule (Pareto's law)

The 80:20 rule encapsulates the truth that many business issues are not uniformly distributed. So, for example, it is typical that 80 per cent of your revenue will come from 20 per cent of your customers; 80 per cent of the aggravation will come from 20 per cent of your customers; 20 per cent of your staff are key to 80 per cent of your business; 80 per cent of personnel management time is spent on 20 per cent of your staff. Wise managers understand Pareto's law and adjust their priorities and investment accordingly.

brilliant tip

Saying no is often more important than saying yes

One of the reasons for having a business strategy is to say no to an opportunity that lands in your lap. It is really hard to turn down easy business, but business that does not fit in with your strategy will stop you pursuing opportunities that do fit with your strategy – so it is not easy business, it is a distraction. Obviously this assumes that you are not desperately short of business!

brilliant tip

Don't neglect your existing customers

Remember that it is far easier to lose an existing customer than it is to find a new one; so invest in caring for your existing customers.

> ### ✦ brilliant tip
>
> **Avoid unpleasant surprises**
>
> The important word here is *surprises*. When you know things are going wrong, let the customer know as soon as possible, do not just hope that things will get better ... they usually get even worse. Customers approached in good time will usually be receptive to a sensible negotiation about managing the problem.

This is a special case of the following more general rule.

> ### ✦ brilliant tip
>
> **Honesty pays**
>
> One of the pleasures of management is that the right thing is usually the smartest thing. If your customer trusts you then everything is so much easier.

> ### ✦ brilliant tip
>
> **Underclaim and overdeliver**
>
> Under pressure to win a sale or soothe an aggrieved customer there is a terrible temptation to quote the best possible delivery time or the lowest possible estimate of extra costs. Try to resist this temptation. In the long term, the smartest thing to do is to add a reasonable contingency and then come in under time and under budget. In many cases lost sales will be more than balanced out by the long-term benefits to your reputation.

Obviously, this advice is predicated on your business being well enough established to be able to afford some short-term loss of sales as an investment for long-term gain. I am sure many readers will find themselves in situations where a customer request to dance naked in the street with a rose in your teeth will be answered by the question, 'What colour rose would you like?'

brilliant tip

Problems are often opportunities

Most customers know that their suppliers will make mistakes. A key issue for many customers is how a supplier handles a mistake. So when your team messes up you must recognise it as an opportunity to extend your relationship with that customer by showing them how well you can retrieve a situation.

I once read an interview with an executive from a car manufacturer discussing his company's efforts to reduce warranty claims. He was asked about his efforts to achieve zero warranty claims for their customers, and he said something like 'of course the ideal number of defects is one ... perfectly handled by the dealer'.

brilliant tip

Talk to the front line

The best way for you to keep your finger on the pulse of your current business is to talk to your staff who directly interact with customers. As just one example, these staff are likely to know about possibilities for selling additional products and services to your existing customers. They are also likely to be aware of what are the 'hot topics' in the customer's mind, which will be excellent indicators of emerging market trends that could well become disruptive forces, or opportunities, for your business.

brilliant tip

Beware the limitations of analogy

One advantage an experienced manager has is the ability to say 'that will not work because I remember when we did ...'. The danger of applying your past experience to draw analogies with a current situation is that circumstances may have changed. In my own area of information technology a common mistake is to say that 'so-and-so has never worked in the past', but computer performance has now improved to an extent where 'so-and-so' is now possible.

brilliant tip

Beware the dangers of extrapolation

It is very easy to assume that a current trend will continue. For example, a market that has been growing at 25 per cent a year can easily lead you to unconsciously assume that the trend will continue, and when it does not you can find yourself overextended. Always be alert for the first signs that a trend is changing and be prepared to (over)react. Always consider investments in the light of the fact that trends may change.

brilliant tip

You often need to overreact to bad news

When things go wrong it is very easy to underestimate how fast things will deteriorate. Always bear in mind that an overreaction seldom does any harm but not reacting fast enough, or strongly enough, can often do irreparable damage.

You often need to overreact to bad news

brilliant tip

Beware diversification

Many small teams will, in business terms, have all their eggs in one basket. In such circumstances there is a great temptation to diversify into other areas. However, diversification tends to reduce marketing focus and it is often better to stick to what you know best. The first thought for diversification should be to apply your core competences to a new, but related, market area.

Summary

Given the importance of business issues I suggest that you make as much time as possible to read the books in the *Suggested reading* section that follows.

Suggested reading

Peeling, Nic (2007) *Brilliant Negotiations: What the Best Negotiators Know, Do and Say*. Harlow, Prentice Hall.
 A very practical, comprehensive book on good negotiating strategies and tactics … well I would say that wouldn't I?

Moore, Geoffrey A. (1997) *Inside the Tornado: Marketing Strategies from Silicon Valley's Cutting Edge*. New York, HarperCollins.

Moore, Geoffrey A. (1999) *Crossing the Chasm: Marketing and Selling High-tech Products to Mainstream Customers*. New York, Harperbusiness.
 Both are 'must reads' if you are in the high-tech industry. I think that many of the ideas are relevant for non-high-tech businesses.

Ries, Al and Jack Trout (1994) *The 22 Immutable Laws of Marketing: Violate Them at Your Own Risk*. New York, Harperbusiness.
 A short, highly readable introduction to the basics of marketing and brands.

Ries, Al and Laura Ries (2000) *The 22 Immutable Laws of Branding*. London, HarperCollinsBusiness.
 A short, highly readable introduction to brand management. Some overlap with *The 22 Immutable Laws of Marketing*.

CHAPTER 8

Managing your organisation

A confession

U ntil this point in the book I think I can reasonably claim I have 'practised what I am preaching'. In this chapter I am suggesting that you 'do as I say, not as I did'. Putting a positive spin on the situation, I am offering you the hard-won experience of many a battle-scarred manager.

Managing your managers

Do not get emotional

No matter how stupid, demotivating, contradictory and small-minded you think your managers are – **STAY CALM**. If you get emotional, you are dead. The problem is that if you are good at your job you are likely to be passionate about it, and in dealing with the rest of your organisation you have to remain cool and cerebral.

In most organisations your bosses will be middle managers. You need to understand that middle managers inhabit a world that is considerably more surreal than any created by J.R.R. Tolkien. Most middle managers know little more than you do about the strategic direction of your organisation and spend their entire lives trying to satisfy the magic processes spun by the wizards from head office. Do not get angry with them, it is probably not their fault. Also remember that, like most people who practise the black arts, they can be very dangerous.

Do not get emotional

Never threaten people's authority

The 'powers that be' will not accept explicit threats to their authority, so you need to achieve your objectives without any crude confrontations.

Good teams are, by their nature, threatening

One of the most depressing facts about being a small team within a larger organisation is that the better your team does, the more it will threaten other people and teams in the organisation. The only way to tackle this is to go beyond the mere avoidance of threatening behaviour and to actually be friendly to those who implicitly feel threatened. The easiest way to do this is to try to get them to feel part of your success. Seek advice and help from people and teams who may feel threatened.

Never, ever, threaten to resign

Just as I advise that you should not give in to threats from your key staff, I think that any sensible organisation should accept your offer of resignation. Threatening to resign is never the way to handle a conflict.

It is possible that you will be put in a position that is completely untenable, in which case you may have to resign. If you are unlucky enough to find yourself in this situation, just go quietly.

Cock-ups are more common than conspiracies
It is very easy to convince yourself that the organisation is out to get you and your team. It is my experience that cock-ups are far more common than conspiracies. Communication within organisations is usually pretty awful. When you start seeing conspiracies behind every tree, it is best to go and have a chat with your boss, or whoever you think is conspiring. I suggest you go in thinking the best ... it's probably just normal organisational incompetence!

It is also important to keep pointing out this viewpoint to your team. There are bound to be plenty of conspiracy theorists in your team. It is important that you provide a calming influence to your team, because the mood will tend to be anti-establishment. Middle managers, personnel managers, accountants, lawyers *et al.* tend not to be bad people; they are usually doing their best under very difficult circumstances. It is important that you try to be tolerant yourself, and try to imbue that tolerance in the team.

> the mood will tend to be anti-establishment

Do not fight battles you cannot win or are not worth the effort
Your team will tend to see every action of 'the system' as an attempt to destroy the team's value. There will occasionally be genuine threats that you have to avert by the more subtle methods I outline below. There will, however, be many issues that you either cannot win or which are not worth the effort to fight. As with so many things, there are only a few things you

can do at any one time. Do not waste your, and the team's, efforts on issues that you cannot win or which are not genuinely life-threatening.

As an example, when introducing ISO 9001 quality processes into the team, my organisation mandated a very unpopular standard format for official reports, and mandated that a particular word processor be used to produce them. The team unanimously wanted me to fight this proposal tooth and nail. I told them bluntly that (a) we would lose, and (b) there were more important issues to win. There were many grumbles, but my view was accepted.

The theory of 'free power'

There are a number of different ways to express this theory. A senior member of an organisation I worked for gave a definition I liked:

It is easier to ask for forgiveness than it is to ask for permission.

Most organisations do not really know how much authority they have delegated to low-level managers. Many organisations help you by saying fine words about empowerment. So in many cases you can just go ahead and do things.

The main disadvantage is that most organisations default to a blame culture, so there will be no comeback if your decision turns out well, but you will get blamed if things go wrong. You have to decide if you care about being blamed. If you just want to do a good job on behalf of your team I suggest you use organisational free power a lot.

A good technique, well backed up by psychology, is to be submissive and apologetic when being blamed. It is really hard, and no fun, to beat up someone when they are grovelling.

One situation when I strongly recommend the use of organisational free power is when the organisation definitely does not want to be asked to give permission. For example, if a staff member asks your permission to do something that is not covered by the rules, then if it is a reasonable request just say yes. In most countries your decision will legally bind your organisation, but the organisation does not want to have to make a decision that may set an organisation-wide precedent. In such cases, the organisation will probably be much happier if you assume the local responsibility for the decision.

Find the wiggle room

Within any organisational process or instruction there is nearly always room for local 'interpretation'. Often it will be possible to show that your local interpretation is in the original spirit of the process or instruction. As an example, when I oversaw the introduction of ISO 9001 quality processes into my team, I got a copy of the actual standard and easily showed that my local interpretations of the corporate quality processes were directly supported by the ISO 9001 document. As the organisation only really cared that the independent quality accreditors would not give me any non-compliances, they left me alone.

Few organisations will fire you for not doing things

In the last resort, rather than threatening to resign, you will usually get away with not carrying out instructions to the letter. Provided you do not rub your managers' noses in the fact that you are being insubordinate, you will usually get away with it.

I strongly recommend that you use this technique very sparingly. Although your superiors may not fire you, they are likely to be able to make life very difficult for you at some time in the future.

Ask for help

When dealing with other departments, such as personnel or finance, a good tactic is to appeal to their professional vanity by asking them how something outside the normal rules can be done. If you seek assistance from someone who has professional pride they will often tell you where the wiggle room is.

Going one step further, if you develop a good relationship with a particular person, then your dealings with that department can be transformed. One way to help develop such a relationship is to be courteous – for example by thanking someone when they have done a good job.

brilliant tip

Don't get too closely associated with a boss. Middle and senior managers often spend a relatively short time in any particular post. If you are too closely allied to an outgoing boss then you may suffer.

Tap into the support subculture

Secretaries and support staff of all kinds are a valuable source of information and help in dealing with the rest of your organisation. If you extend my advice about being courteous to your team members to people outside your team then you will find it relatively easy to tap into the support subculture. You will find that stopping for a chat with secretaries and support staff is not only very interesting, it can also be very informative, and that such people often have some power to help you, and always have great power to hinder you.

Initiatives

Organisations seem very keen these days on buzzword-based initiatives. Knowledge management, quality, total quality, re-engineering, benchmarking and the like all seem to be rolled out at regular intervals. In addition, there are the annual processes such as business planning to be dealt with, which seem to change their form each year. How does one handle them?

> organisations seem very keen on buzzword-based initiatives

Be first or last

There is an advantage in being first to embrace an initiative. You will get brownie points. You will also have the maximum say in setting the interpretation of the initiative. Otherwise, let the other suckers get all the bugs out and do it at the last possible moment.

Hijack the initiative

Initiatives often come with some sort of funding, even if it is only some allowance of time for you and your staff. Consider if you can use the initiative to make some change that you wanted to make anyway. As an example, many people use the introduction of quality processes to re-engineer a slicker set of procedures in the team.

The great advantage of such an approach is that the team is likely to be more motivated in implementing the initiative if there is some direct benefit to the team. It is my view that the skilful manager can turn almost all initiatives to some advantage. This avoids the difficult situation where you are trying to get the team to implement an initiative that your staff know you do not really believe in.

Use the initiative to negotiate a change in your targets

It is often possible to use an initiative to negotiate a change to your existing targets with your boss. Your boss may well accept that the new priority implied by the latest initiative means that existing priorities have to be reassessed.

Do initiatives 'well enough'

Avoid the mistake of overdoing the level of effort to implement an initiative. If you put it positively – that you are looking to get the maximum 'bangs for the buck' from the initiative – this will not be seen as a criticism of the initiative.

Your personal bonus and targets

This is a very dangerous subject. Your staff will know that you are likely to have targets to meet. They will suspect, often correctly, that these targets are very crude measures of performance, and they will suspect that you are allowing the pursuit of your bonus to unduly affect your behaviour.

Tell the team what your targets and bonuses are
There is no better way to defuse the suspicions of your team than being totally open. I also suggest that you acknowledge that the smart thing to do is to keep 'them' happy by hitting as many of the targets as possible. Although the targets are likely to be crude, it is usually possible to achieve them without doing any significant damage to other more important performance indicators. If the targets are really damaging I suggest you discuss with the team the extent to which you should balance the targets against the other more important factors – remembering that you cannot just ignore the organisation's targets, no matter how stupid they are.

In Chapter 4 I recommended that you use part of your bonus to sponsor team social events – after all, it is their efforts you are being rewarded for.

Summary

Here are the four most important messages from this chapter for the brilliant manager.

1   Do not get emotional with your bosses. Passion is a great attribute of a leader, but a terrible way to manage the rest of your organisation.

2   Use the 'free power' within the organisation. It is better to apologise after the event than ask for permission beforehand.

3   Find the wiggle room within your organisation's processes. Best of all, get a good working relationship with other departments in your organisation, particularly finance, contracts, legal and personnel.

4   Try to hijack your organisation's initiatives to implement improvements within your team.

CHAPTER 9

Key management themes

There are several key themes that underpin all of management. Some of them have been touched on in earlier chapters. This chapter brings them to the surface and looks at them as a whole.

Managing the dependencies

Although this book discusses different aspects of management in isolation, you must consider them as a whole. Your leadership style must be appropriate to the culture you are creating. The team's culture must be appropriate to the sort of business you are in, and the customers you sell products and services to. Your business must fit your team's capabilities. Your team's organisation and processes must fit the culture and your business. The team culture must be matched to your organisation's culture. Your recruitment process must match the culture and the business needs … and so on. Managing these dependencies well is one of the aspects that separate the brilliant manager from the good manager.

The golden rule

Your own personal behaviour sets the example that your team will follow. There is no way I can overemphasise the importance of this golden rule. It does not matter how well you can talk the talk, what matters is that you can walk the walk. The power of the golden rule comes into its own if you have strong principles on which to base your actions.

Principles and integrity

Management is so much easier if you want to use your power to make things happen. It is also much easier if you have a clear view of right from wrong. If you have a strong foundation on which to base your behaviour, you can behave naturally and, naturally, you will behave consistently. From my personal observation I believe that the 'right thing' is nearly always the smart thing. Most people can use their intellect to deduce what the right thing to do is in most circumstances. The golden rule will ensure that those managers who behave in a principled way will be respected. Your staff will not respect you less, and may even respect you more, if they know that you are using your intellect, rather than your nature, to behave well.

The straight bat

Another example of the application of integrity is to use what I call *the straight bat* approach to tricky management problems. In situations where you are unsure of people's motives or reactions, I recommend that you play the situation from a principled view of trying to do the right thing. There are three great advantages of this approach. First, from my own personal experience, it is as effective, and often more effective, than more sophisticated tactics. Second, it is very easy to defend your actions, and often people will respond to honesty with honesty. Last, if everything goes pear-shaped and you get shot, then you can console yourself with the thought that you tried to do the right thing and that your problems are not the result of playing the politics wrong.

> your problems are not the result of playing the politics wrong

Principles and passion

Managers with strong principles are often very passionate about the things they are trying to achieve. In many circumstances passion is a positive attribute of a manager: for example, it can be a powerful motivator for a team. There is, however, a flip side that the principled, passionate manager must beware of. Passionate people can get emotional in circumstances when the more dispassionate manager can remain cool and detached. There are times when the cool and detached approach is essential: for example, knowing when to cut one's losses, and dealing with your superiors.

Managing the extremes

Managers must accept that they will often have to occupy the extremes of spectra. The last section described how brilliant managers must utilise, at the appropriate times, both the extremes of passion and detachment. Previous chapters have described how managers may often have to react hard and fast to some situations, whereas other cases will benefit from what I called benign neglect. Almost every area described in this book, from culture to marketing to people management, advises that you consider adopting extreme positions. Management is not for the faint-hearted!

brilliant tip

Tell staff how they can increase their value to your organisation. It is unfair to deny such constructive feedback to your team members.

The courage to be ruthless

One of the examples of extremes that may have surprised you is the mixture of kindness and ruthlessness that I recommend in areas such as people management. One of the commonest mistakes I see in otherwise brilliant managers is that they are too kind. It is my view that in many circumstances, kindness inappropriately applied can in reality be unkind, cruel and bad management. Take as an example a seemingly kind decision to keep a long-term underperformer in your team. Someone underperforming is quite likely unhappy, because most people like to do a good job and to be appreciated. That person might well be underperforming because they do not fit into your team or are doing work for which they have little talent. They are a danger to the long-term survival of the team. Others of your staff are likely to suffer increased pressure covering for the under-performer's lack of performance. All in all, your kindness in this situation may make everyone unhappy, so your kindness may in truth be more to do with lack of courage.

Respect, fair play and courtesy

The word *ruthless* is often associated in people's minds with the phrase *ruthless bastard*. Although I am encouraging you to consider extreme behaviour when appropriate, I also advocate that such extremes of behaviour bring with them a duty to be consistent, fair-minded, respectful and courteous. It is again my view that not only is such behaviour right, it is also smart. A courteous request usually achieves more than a curt command. Fair-mindedness and consistency will allow ruthless behaviour to be applied appropriately without creating a climate of fear.

Judgement

The sorts of behaviour I am recommending in this book will go a long way to gaining the respect of your staff. There is, however, one aspect of gaining respect that I have not so far mentioned – judgement. To be a good manager you must make lots of good decisions. No matter how principled, courteous and consistent a manager you are, you have got to be good at your job. Good judgement is essential in a good manager; without that I suggest you look for another job where you will do less harm.

Dangers of overworking

I have alluded a number of times to the extreme pressures that most managers work under. There is a great danger that one of your responses to these pressures will be to regularly work very long hours. I have fallen into this trap myself and when I eventually broke out of the long hours habit was able to see that, for me, the effects had been:

- I was so tired that my judgement was very severely impaired;
- I worked very inefficiently and got more work done when I reduced my working hours;
- I made too many mistakes;
- I squeezed out essential activities such as communications and strategy;
- I lost the ability to say no, so did more work and attended more meetings than I should have;
- I set a bad example to my team who started to copy my work patterns;
- I got bad tempered and moody;
- My home life suffered very badly.

If you have got the long hours habit, try an experiment and cut your hours down to see if things improve for you.

Pareto's law

The 80:20 rule applies to almost all aspects of a manager's job. Unfortunately it is all too often ignored in setting priorities. One particular trap is to spend too much effort on the new, sexy issues and ignore the boring stuff that pays your salary.

Remember to protect your existing customer base; grow your

the 80:20 rule applies
to almost all aspects of
a manager's job

existing product lines; sell to your existing customers first; look after your key staff; and make sure your key staff are deployed on the most important jobs.

Focus, focus and focus

The three most important techniques for making good decisions are focus, focus and focus. In many areas of management you must appreciate that only a few things can be achieved. For example, a product positioning can only include a few competitive differentiators; a business strategy can only achieve a few things in a year; a team culture can only have a few extreme aspects; and you can only win a few battles with your management.

Play to your strengths

A common mistake managers make is to seek to achieve an idealised situation. You have to work with what you have to hand. It is no good you pretending you are good at things you are poor at – better to delegate those tasks to someone with more talent. Organise your team around the staff you actually have. Develop a business strategy that builds on the existing strengths of your current products and services, your current staff's expertise, and your current customer base. Deploy your staff on jobs that play to their talents.

Delegation and micro-management do not mix

Most managers know the importance of delegation, but few managers understand how to delegate properly. Choosing what jobs to delegate, to whom, with an upfront agreement as to the

It is no good pretending you are good at things you are poor at

levels of control over the delegated task, have been discussed in some detail in previous chapters. The need to allow people to do things differently from yourself and the need to let people learn from their mistakes make delegation one of the hardest tasks a manager will face. You have to avoid micro-management, while remaining in overall control. Unless you trust your staff to work well without detailed supervision, they will never develop the confidence and experience to be worthy of your trust.

Perceptions are the only reality

Marketing people should understand this maxim, but it applies to all your activities. For example, if you are perceived as being unfair then the reality is unimportant; you must always address the perception. Do not make the mistake of blaming anyone except yourself for wrong perceptions. You must listen to your customers, staff, other groups in your organisation, suppliers and collaborators so that you know how you, your team and its products and services are perceived. Too many managers are one-way communication devices; you must learn personally, and as a team, to listen.

By default you have created a blame culture

A very common perception that managers find difficult to accept is that their team has a blame culture. This is easier to understand once you accept that you have to go to extreme lengths to avoid creating a blame culture. Are you willing to reward someone who made an honourable failure? Are you willing to allow people to have the responsibility for making decisions and then you accept the blame with your superiors when things go wrong? Are you willing to genuinely praise people who bring you bad news? Can you give constructive criticism with no blame at all? Are you still sure you have not created a blame culture?

This is really important because if you want your team to push their performance to the extremes, to take calculated risks and to embrace change and other challenges, then you have to avoid creating a blame culture.

You have to go to extreme lengths to avoid creating a blame culture

By default your team is regarded as arrogant

Another common perception of a good team is that it is insular and arrogant. Unless you are overtly open and conciliatory to your superiors and other teams in your organisation, that is how you will be viewed.

Many of your problems are in your head

You must face the fact that you can do most things that you need to. Your organisation, your customers, your staff and the personnel department are not stopping you. If you face the problem, and all the knock-on effects that your decision will produce, then in most cases you will be able to do what you want to.

Value diversity

Sometimes I think that some managers would be happier if all their staff were obedient company clones. To build good teams you need a wide pool of staff with different talents to draw upon. You may need creative people, project managers, good writers, good presenters, good reviewers, analysts, professional workers ... the list is endless. Each different sort of personality and skill-set brings its

> you will naturally get interpersonal tensions

own specific problems, and the better the skill, the more extreme the problems tend to be. Good managers should delight in the diversity and excellence of their staff and know that one of their main jobs is to manage the problems that come with any diverse group of talented people.

In any group of talented people you will naturally get interpersonal tensions. It is important that you show you respect all the different skills and personalities in your team. In this way the golden rule will help you create a culture where people respect each other's talents, even if they do not like each other.

Often you have to give before you can receive

In many areas you will have to take a lead, leaving yourself somewhat exposed. You have to give trust before people have earned that trust. You have to show you trust your team before they will trust you. The same is true of respect; you have to give people respect before they will respect you. Honesty is the same; often you have to behave honestly for an extended period of time before people will treat you with similar honesty.

Humility

I should like to conclude this chapter with a warning about the dangers from your own ego. No one likes to be asked to do something by someone who would not be willing to do that job themselves. In the fast-paced, high-pressured, quick-fire world that many managers inhabit it is all too easy to lose any sense of humility. One extreme view of a manager's role is as a servant of the team. You are there to create an environment in which they can get on and do the real work, such as shielding them from the crap that falls from above, fighting petty bureaucracy and making sure the money keeps rolling in. A little humility never did a manager any harm at all.

Suggested reading

McCormack, Mark H. (2001) *What They Still Don't Teach You at Harvard Business School*. New York, Bantam Books.
    A streetwise, and at times cynical, set of business and management techniques from a highly articulate, self-made businessman. I found this a very influential book.

CHAPTER 10

Management master-class

This chapter contains the most probing questions about management I have ever been asked. It will give you the final touches you need to set you well on the way to becoming a brilliant manager.

Is project management the same as team management?

I think the simple answer is not really – team management and project management are radically different. An outstanding project manager is not guaranteed to make a good team manager, and vice versa.

So what are the big differences between a brilliant project manager and a brilliant team manager?

- Project managers do not have to be strong on strategy. The project objectives provide the target that the project manager must lead their team to achieve.

- Many brilliant project managers have dictatorial leadership styles. Few brilliant team managers use a dictatorial approach.

- Project managers must have an eye for detail. When a project manager transfers to team management this can easily lead to excessive micro-management.

- Project managers build team cultures that are time limited.

A team manager needs to build a long-lived, less single-minded culture.

● Project managers must have an innate understanding of scheduling issues. This is not as essential in a team manager.

● Good project managers can get away with acting as if the end justifies the means, whereas this would undermine the integrity of a team manager.

● Project managers will be forgiven for being self-, or project-centred, whereas a team manager needs to build long-term relationships with people outside the team.

● Brilliant project managers are good at task allocation, but seldom delegate their own duties. Team managers must be good delegators.

How do you go about turning round a failing team?

This is one of the most extreme, and hence exciting, situations a manager can find themselves in.

The team must feel you know exactly what has to be done and what part each of them must play.

The five key steps to turning round a failing team are these.

1 Understand the terms of reference that your superiors have imposed on you. How much time do you have? What is the minimum that would be considered a successful turnaround?

2 Understand the team's problems … fast!

3 Decide if the team can be saved.

4 Institute emergency actions.

5 Create and implement a recovery strategy, and initial plan.

I could tell you a lot of sad stories about people who didn't do step 1 properly. It is dreadful to think you have turned a team around, or to be well on the way to success, only to find that your superiors disagree and pull the plug. Step 1 will help you avoid snatching defeat from the jaws of victory.

There are two aspects to step 2. The first is to find out whose opinions you can trust and then listen to them. If you ask a lot of people who they trust you will find that a few names keep being mentioned … trust them. The second thing you must do is understand the finances of the team. The accounts may well be in a mess, but you must find out the true financial underpinnings of the team.

Step 3 is often missed out – as you have been brought in to turn the team around, you need to try. It is however your duty to disband the team if that is the best all-round solution.

The most common emergency action is to downsize the team as this is the fastest way to improve the finances. Step 4 can be tricky, but you should find that things improve rapidly – morale will lift as the remaining staff will see themselves as survivors and will start to believe that the problem has been brought under control.

To use a medical analogy, if step 4 involved stabilising the patient, step 5 is about establishing a course of treatment that will lead to the patient's full recovery. Every recovery strategy is different, but the amount of work you need to put into it is the same – you will almost certainly have to ask for heroic efforts from your team and you must set the example. The good news here is that it's an ideal opportunity to use your leadership skills to set a really positive tone for the future.

brilliant impact

Set your team an achievable but challenging first target, so they quickly see themselves (and you) as winners, not losers.

Step 6: leave

Many organisations will choose to change the team leader once the turnaround is complete. There are good reasons for this. Turnaround managers are often a special breed of person who will not handle a less exciting management role well. In addition, a turnaround manager will often have had to be very ruthless and demanding, and it may well be appropriate to change leadership to give a new leader a fresh start. You may want to discuss your future after a turnaround before you take on the job. If you know that you must leave after the turnaround then you can manage your exit with style, and hopefully move on within the organisation to another exciting challenge.

What are the minimum essentials to be a brilliant manager?

My minimal list would be as follows.

- *Set a good example*. Obviously you must obey the golden rule ('you will be judged by your actions, not by your words, and your actions set the example for your team to follow') so that your own behaviour sets a good example. This will allow you to set high standards.

- *Create a brilliant strategy*. If you are to be a good leader you must be leading your team in a sensible direction, so creating a great strategy has to be near the top of your list. You then have to communicate that strategy to your team.

- *Understand the finances*. Keep a close eye on the bottom line of your team.

- *Act with integrity*. Your team will forgive you a lot if you have integrity.

- *Be courageous*. You must have the courage to tackle under-performance and misconduct.

- *Be decisive.* You must have the courage to be decisive; you need to be a good listener to ensure that your decisions are well-informed; and you need the judgement to make lots of right decisions.
- *Don't be a bully.*
- *Don't blame people.*

What's the worst and most frequent mistake to make?

Trusting the wrong people. Be clever here – watch those around you carefully and you will quickly find out who people in the team feel comfortable turning to for advice. These are the people that you should seek advice from too.

What's the easiest mistake to make?

Wanting to be 'one of the gang' and liked by all. To be a brilliant manager you must set yourself apart. Few people enjoy loneliness, so the desire to be a member of the team as well as the boss is a very easy mistake to make.

What are the three worst qualities a manager can have?

Obviously this is a very subjective list, but I would have my top three as:

- dishonesty, including lying;
- cowardice, including not addressing poor performance and misconduct;
- poor judgement.

How can you improve your performance?

Seek feedback from your team members, your peers and your superiors. You will find that many people will give you constructive criticism. When receiving feedback you must be very careful not to get defensive and to keep justifying yourself. It isn't the reality that matters, it is people's perceptions you want to listen to.

When a person leaves your team, I suggest you give them an exit interview. As well as finding out their reasons for leaving, you can probe for their perceptions of your organisation and your team. There is no reason why you cannot also ask for their views of you personally. On such an occasion you are uniquely placed to receive a frank and uninhibited assessment of your strengths and weaknesses.

A key technique is to be able to develop an analytical approach to your job. Take the time to regularly do a mental debrief on the recent past. What went well, what went badly, and most importantly why did things go well or badly. This is the process that led to me developing my ideas of what makes a brilliant manager. In this book I obviously have looked at generally applicable principles. You can use the same technique to work out what is the style, and what are the techniques, that can make you the best possible manager.

> develop an analytical approach to your job

Is ambition a good or bad thing?

The reason that many people do not like working for an ambitious boss is that such bosses tend to behave in ways that promote themselves, rather than doing the best for their team and their organisation. As an example, ambitious people will seldom let the team take the credit or accept any blame personally. It is a very sophisticated ambitious person who behaves with integrity and is a good team player, in order to get promoted because they have done a good job.

There is a good side to ambition and a dark side. The good side is seeking promotion because you want to do the job that is available at the higher grade. If you want to lead a team of people then you will want to be promoted to be a team leader. If you want to influence the strategy of your organisation you will aspire to a senior position. The dark side is wanting the kudos, money and power that comes with promotion. There is nothing wrong with enjoying such aspects, as long as you do not become a slave to such pleasures.

Being slightly morbid, put yourself in the following situation: you are 80 years old and your doctor has told you that you only have a few weeks left to live. You sit down in your favourite chair and open a really good bottle of wine, and you then look back over your life. What things will make you proud and what things now seem unimportant? Thinking now about what you really value is much better than waiting until it is too late. This leads on to the next question.

Is management important?

Brilliant managers have a very significant positive impact on the quality of life of the people in their team. As a profession that makes a difference to people. I do not think it is silly to compare managers to parents, teachers, nurses and the like. As such, I feel an 80-year-old retired manager should be proud if they felt they had been a good manager.

Brilliant management has a very significant effect on the profit and growth of a team. I have not succeeded in finding any research into the performance impact of good team managers, but I suspect most readers of this book believe that it is significant. From my own personal experience, I have taken over a team that had a sound business, but was not particularly well managed. Within a year of taking over, the financial performance of the team, measured by its profit per person in the team, rose by over 20 per cent and I was also able to grow what had been a static turnover by 100 per cent in 3 years.

How do you handle office politics?

I really wish I could say that you can just ignore office politics, but your team will expect you to be able to hold your own. From my own observations I offer the following advice.

- *Behave with integrity.* This is often the smartest move. If you gain a reputation for telling the truth, not undermining other people in your organisation, and living the values of your organisation, then your superiors are much more likely to back you if you find yourself in a political conflict.

- *Be a good team player.* Having a reputation as a good team player who works well with people outside your local team offers you a very strong defence against political pressures. The more senior members of your organisation are likely to want to reward people who put the wider interests of the organisation ahead of parochial issues. Because many of the enthusiastic players of office politics are pursuing very personal agendas you will probably find that you will have senior-level support if you do not project a local perspective.

- *Be aware.* You need to be aware of what's going on in your organisation. Knowledge *is* power.

- *Gain respect.* You need to know what behaviours will be expected by your superiors and develop sufficient of them to be highly regarded. Highly regarded people will attract more high-level support in an organisation than less well-regarded people.

- *Build a power base.* The easiest way to do this is to develop a network of contacts who respect you. Being respectful to people, and a willingness to be helpful to others, is a very good start. Your contacts will often support you in a political conflict and will also be a great source of intelligence. Be generous by sharing what you know with your contacts.
- *Don't overreact.* Your superiors are unlikely to tolerate an over-the-top retaliation.

How do you set the pay of your staff?

The first rule of pay setting to be aware of is:

Your staff will be most affected by comparison with other team members, second by others in the organisation, and last by comparison with others outside the organisation.

This means that getting the pay differentials right within the team should be your highest priority. Of course, pay tends to be just one dimension of an organisation's reward structure, so you might think that the previous sentence should read 'getting the reward differentials right within the team should be your highest priority'. Unfortunately, people tend to compare each individual element of their reward structure, so you have to get pay differentials right, and you have to make promotion decisions correctly, and you have to implement bonuses and other incentives fairly ... and so on. Consequently, I will deal with pay in isolation.

> assume that most staff will have some idea of what others are paid

Even if you work in an organisation that tries to keep the details of people's pay in the strictest confidence, I would recommend that you assume that most of your team will have some idea of what others are paid.

The process I recommend for pay setting is as follows.

First, talk to every member of your team about their pay aspirations
This will alert you to those people whose aspirations need to be moderated, and you will probably be pleasantly surprised how modest many people's aspirations are. You will also find out if there are promises on pay that have been made to people in the past – because people are naturally indignant when they feel that promises have been broken.

Sit down with a list of your staff and work out what you would ideally like to pay them
To do this properly you will need access, if possible, to the pay levels of staff outside your team, and also some idea of what some of your people would be paid by your competitors. Remember that pay levels advertised in the press tend to be significantly higher than the average levels paid in your industry. Hopefully your personnel department will be able to provide you with up-to-date data, but if they cannot, you will have to do your own research.

Following this process will help you set the right relativities within your team.

Try to get everyone as near to the idealised pay as your organisation allows
If you are not given complete autonomy to set pay levels in your team, then it may be time to brush up on your political skills. Having done your homework, you will find it easier to argue for your people.

Personally, I think it is worth telling the team the process you and the organisation use to set pay levels. If you do not say, then people will suspect the worst.

Let people know individually what their likely pay rise is before they get official notification

This will allow you to soften the blow for those who are not getting the pay rise they hoped for. It will also maximise the beneficial effects when someone gets more than they were expecting.

I realise that the process I am recommending here is time-consuming, but pay is such a powerful demotivator (it is seldom a motivator) that I think you have little choice but to find the time.

A common misconception about pay is that it is a reward for good performance. Pay should be appropriate to the value of the person to the organisation. If you wish to use money as a reward, then consider some form of one-off bonus, not an increase in salary.

You also need to remember that you can seriously damage someone by paying them too much. Ultimately, someone who is overpaid is going to disappoint their organisation, so the person will probably face grief as a result, and, in extremis, could end up losing their job. They will also adapt their lifestyle to their salary, so will face some significant pain if they eventually have to return to a more appropriate salary.

The final point I will make about pay is to quote two well-researched but surprising statistics.

1   For professionals, such as computer programmers, the difference in productivity between the best and worst performers is typically 10:1. In my personal experience this is an underestimate, because there are many jobs that the best performers can do that lesser performers would fail to finish.

2   In the USA, *Management Accounting* reports that the difference in salary between outstanding employees and average employees is just 3 per cent.

I suggest you try to beat the 3 per cent differential, both by rewarding the better performers and by offering below-average performers little or no pay increases. You may find it surprisingly difficult to hold back the pay of below-average performers. Often your organisation will make it very hard for you to do this, but I think it is worth the fight. You will often be told that you will make matters worse by demotivating such staff. In my view such staff are seldom very motivated, so you will do little harm; you will clearly show that you do not think their perform-

ensure that you reward achievement and effort, not appearances

ance matches their salary; you increase the chance that they will voluntarily leave the organisation; and finally, you will improve the morale of the better staff who will see that they get a proper differential for the extra value they deliver to your organisation.

One issue that makes staff particularly twitchy is that they may suspect that you pay people for how they look, act and talk, rather than based on what value they actually deliver to the team. You need to ensure that you reward achievement and effort, not appearances.

What's the best way to promote someone?

Many organisations have an explicit stratification that reflects a person's status. Promotion from one level to the next has as much, if not more, effect on morale as pay does. Promoting the wrong people will seriously undermine the team's trust in your judgement, as well as seriously demotivating your team.

I would suggest you check any proposed promotions with a few people whose judgement you trust. The greatest danger is that you promote someone who looks better to their superiors than they do to their peers and their subordinates. Another danger is that you promote people because they have worked on projects that you are particularly interested in.

How do you handle harassment?

Distinguish the sad from the bad

Most harassment falls into one of two very distinct camps, which I label the *sad* and the *bad*. The *sad* is due to the inadequacies of the person doing the harassing. If someone is sexually immature or inadequate then they can make members of the opposite sex feel very uncomfortable. If someone comes from a culture or upbringing where intolerance was rife, then they may well pick up intolerant speech patterns and habits, whilst not being malicious. The *bad* are those who use sex or other forms of harassment, such as bullying, to impose their will and power over others. In my view there is nothing wrong in being reasonably tolerant of the sad, but the bad should be confronted. There will however be many cases where it will be very hard for the person being harassed to know if they should confront the person doing the harassment. For example, if a sad harasser is making life intolerable for someone, there may be no alternative but to confront the harassment. It is also worth bearing in mind that some sad harassers will respond positively to being confronted. But how do you confront harassment?

Confronting unacceptable harassment

Probably my most controversial view is that people who lodge formal complaints of harassment usually suffer greatly for their courage, and I would recommend that this be absolutely the last resort. The most effective approach I have seen is for the harassed person to firmly and unemotionally confront the harasser on each and every occasion of harassment, *and tell them to stop.* Given that 'bad' harassment is usually about power and hatred, this approach gives the harasser the minimum gratification from their harassment.

As a manager, you should confront harassment within your team, whenever you become aware of it – and the boss telling someone to stop it can often have more effect than the subject of the harassment can have. You also have the advantage that as a manager you will be in less danger if you have to lodge a formal complaint of harassment on behalf of one of your staff, than the subject of the harassment would be if they had to make the complaint personally.

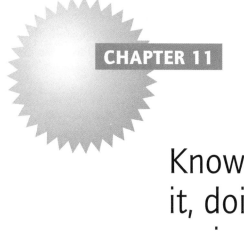

CHAPTER 11

Knowing it, doing it, saying it

I am very aware of the limitations of this book. It's very easy to discuss management in principle – but not always as easy to apply this in the real world. To help bridge the gap between theory and practice here are a number of real-life scenarios complete with discussion of how you might deal with these situations.

Scenario 1

A member of your team who I will call 'A' complains about sexual harassment by a person I will call 'B'

Here is a situation that probably strikes terror into the heart of every manager.

Let's start with what you say to 'A' when the allegation is first made. The important thing here is not to say too much until you have talked to the relevant authorities and done some investigations. On the other hand, if things turn nasty then everthing you did, *and did not,* say may well be used in evidence against you. At the initial meeting I would suggest that you do the following.

- Collect as much information from the complainant as possible. Go somewhere private and try to get all the information you can. Do not be embarrassed about asking specific questions concerning dates, words used, actual physical contact alleged, etc., because such information is key to checking the veracity of the complainant's allegations. In asking specific questions, you need to avoid going into such detail that you might appear to be a voyeur.

- You need to assure the complainant that your organisation takes such complaints very seriously indeed and that you will immediately seek advice from your personnel department, and that you will read up on the company procedures to ensure that the complaint is dealt with properly.

- Ask the complainant if they want you to do anything immediately: you need to check that they are able to cope with the current situation for a few more days as you set the wheels in motion.

I would suggest that you beware the following.

- While expressing sympathy for the complainant's distress you must not give any indication that you accept that the complaint is justified. You must remember that you owe it to 'B' to accept that they are innocent until proved guilty (I am talking in moral terms here rather than in purely legal terms).

- Do not show any signs of hostility.

- Do not try to talk the complainant out of making their complaint; neither must you be seen to be encouraging them to make a formal complaint.

- Try to avoid promising to do anything specific until you have had the opportunity to talk to your personnel advisers.

- Avoid all physical contact or anything that might *in any way* be misinterpreted as inappropriate behaviour.

Unsurprisingly, the next step is to read the company procedures and then alert your personnel staff and seek their advice. Let me make it quite clear, you must do precisely what they say: anything else leaves you personally exposed.

It is difficult to give much more general advice because you will be in the hands of your organisation's processes for handling such complaints. There are, however, three areas where I have personally found that the manager can help.

If possible, find out what the complainant wants to be done

This is not as simple as it sounds. Some staff will just want the harassment to stop. Others will feel that they have to make a formal complaint to stop 'B' doing it to anyone else. It may be that 'A' is seeking retribution and wants to see 'B' punished. It may be that 'A' feels that they deserve some form of compensation. Knowing what 'A' wants to happen can have a material effect on the way the organisation handles such a complaint, and often organisations fail to discover this crucial piece of information.

Check the complainant can cope with the stress

Many complainants find the process of making a complaint enormously stressful, and you have a duty to ensure that they can cope. It may be that at a later date 'A' will change their view of what they want as an outcome and may want you, or someone else, to confront 'B', with the objective of stopping the alleged harassment. Once the wheels of the formal

> many complainants find the process of making a complaint enormously stressful

process have started to grind, it can be very difficult to stop them. If, however, you speak up loudly then you will usually be listened to.

Ensure that the accused person is also treated fairly

Many organisations unintentionally tend to favour the complainant. In the interests of justice, you should be prepared to insist that the person being accused is not assumed to be guilty without there being a strong case proven against them.

Scenario 2

You have been brought in to turn around a failing team and you find the main problem is that a key creative person has left

This is a very difficult problem. Assuming that you are not going to redirect the activities of the team so that the creative role is less important, the steps I would recommend are these.

- The first thing to do is to check that there is no one else in the team who has the potential to step into that person's shoes.

- If there is no such person then you need to work out how much you can afford to pay a replacement.

- It can then be worth contacting the person who left and testing out whether they might be willing to return – why had they left? You can tell them that you are now in charge and things are changing. If they are not willing to return, you could ask them if they know anyone who might be interested in their old job.

- It is often more successful to try to offer an opportunity to an up-and-coming talent than to try to recruit someone who has already made their name.

- Find out who in the team has a good network of contacts and use these to approach likely candidates directly.

- Last, you can use advertisements and headhunters. I suggest that you include something in advertisements along the lines that creative ability is as important as a long track record, and also include a wide salary range.

Scenario 3

A customer is making unreasonable demands on one of your staff

Obviously you will do everything you can to protect your staff from unreasonable demands, but, in extremis, you will have to decide whether your staff or your customer comes first. However, the cunning manager can usually avoid having to make such a black or white stand.

- You can talk to the staff member and discuss whether there is any way that they can cope with the unreasonable demands. Remember there is nothing wrong with bribery – you can offer time off once the job for the customer is over; you can offer a bonus; and you can offer non-cash inducements.

- You can talk to the customer and cunningly get them to behave more reasonably. For example, 'I am worried that the pressure this work is putting my staff under might prejudice the quality of the job we are doing for you – is there any way we can reduce that pressure?'

- You can rotate your staff through the post that deals with the difficult customer.

If you have to make a choice between your staff and that customer there is no shame in recognising the power of the customer – an obnoxious but marginal customer makes it much easier to put your staff first. Staff will realise that they may suffer if a key customer account is lost and so may well accept you backing an important, but difficult, customer.

> there is no shame in recognising the power of the customer

Scenario 4

One of your staff comes to you and says they cannot cope with their work

You should be very grateful that they had the courage to come and tell you. It is important that you handle this in a way that will encourage, rather than discourage, other people to do the same.

There are three likely scenarios.

- First, the person basically has too much to do and has reached the state of the rabbit mesmerised by the oncoming headlights of a car. The obvious solution is to go through the person's workload and prioritise it so they know which items they can drop or transfer to someone else.

- Second, the person cannot do part of their job properly. This might be something as simple as the need for some training, but more likely they are doing a job for which they have little aptitude. Usually a change of job is the best solution.

- Last, it is a cry for help that relates to something other than the person's work. You need to probe for the real problem.

Scenario 5

The team has an urgent deadline and people are having to work extremely long hours to try to meet it
There are lots of things you can do to help.

- Even if you are not working on the project then it is worth working long hours yourself, though I would suggest that you do your own work rather than look over the shoulders of the workers.

- You can provide a supportive environment. For example, you can make sure that everyone eats regularly and go to get the food yourself. The boss as the servant of the team is a powerful symbol.

- You can act as support to the project manager. With everyone working flat out it is very easy for the wood to be lost for the trees. You can get everyone together occasionally to check that the work is being done efficiently. You may also be able to use your outside perspective to spot how extra resource could be deployed, and to identify risks that are being missed.

- You can identify when people are too tired to work efficiently and send them home to sleep – by taxi if necessary.
- Perhaps most importantly you need to take a lead if it is clear the deadline is going to be missed and either deliver less on time or negotiate a sensible extension.
- When it's all over don't forget to reward and thank people.

Scenario 6

You have a staff member who works incredibly long hours and refuses to slow down

Ultimately it is an individual's right to set their own priorities. If their work patterns are causing them to make too many mistakes or are causing anti-social behaviour such as extreme shortness of temper, then you will have to insist that they work less hard, but in most such instances this will not be the case. There are a couple of techniques I have had success with. You can try occasionally coming in late to the office and sending them home. You can try persuading them to take a day off a month – often such people can manage their diaries to block out a complete day to spend with their families.

Scenario 7

There is a major change in office accommodation about to happen

Facetiously I might suggest you reach for a crash helmet! There is almost nothing that arouses stronger passions than changes to office accommodation. The physical working environment is rightly felt by staff to be critical to both their productivity and quality of life. Add to this the less noble feeling of territoriality and status, and you have a potentially explosive mixture.

A major change in office accommodation is about to happen

Techniques I have seen work include the following.

- Find a mother or father figure who is liked and respected by the team and put them in charge. People will tend to behave much better if such a person is controlling the change. An alternative is for you to take charge and thus put your full authority behind the decisions.

- Make sure that the principles of accommodation allocation are clearly articulated and rigorously applied. If accommodation is allocated by job requirements, and has no relationship to status, then say so and stick to it.

- Make sure people have plenty of time to get used to the proposed plan. Never jump the allocation on your team at the last minute. It takes time for people to adjust to change.

Scenario 8

A long-term underperformer is moved into your team

A proper, and cunning, move is to ask personnel for their advice on how to handle the person concerned. This will make it easier if you have to get them involved later on.

The first thing I would say is that you should approach the person with an open mind. It is not impossible that someone has been in the wrong job or in the wrong environment.

I would suggest being very precise in your management of the person. Make it clear what is expected of them and try to set realistic, measurable objectives.

If you have concerns with their performance then the $64,000 question is whether you should deal with the issue in exactly the same way as you would with any other staff member. In particular, you will have a clear idea of how much time you would normally allow someone to address problems before you decide you must institute the processes your organisation has in place for handling underperformers – *are you any less patient for a persistent underperformer?* I suggest you ask personnel to decide how long you have to give the person to improve.

Scenario 9

A worker comes to you and says they think they've drilled into asbestos

There are some issues you cannot afford to take any chances with, and the top of this list is health and safety. Unless you have very strong reasons to believe that the worker is mistaken, you should immediately clear and seal off the affected area. Then you should notify your health and safety people. If you cannot get an instant response you should immediately escalate the issue within the health and safety department, and if this does not yield quick results then escalate it up your management chain.

Scenario 10

You suspect one of your staff is taking kickbacks from a supplier

One of the things you need to understand is when to act on your own responsibility and when to call in the 'experts'. This is one of the cases where you should hotfoot it to your personnel department, which may then refer you to security or directly to the police. One rule of thumb is that anything that could possibly end up in court should go straight to the experts, whose advice you must follow to the letter.

Scenario 11

The person you are using as your internal operations manager resigns

If there is an obvious replacement then this is a no-brainer. The problem comes when you have no obvious replacement. Usually it is best to leave the position vacant, covering the role yourself until something turns up. It takes some confidence to leave an intractable problem alone 'until something turns up' – but it is often better than making a bad decision.

Scenario 12

An important project has hit major problems

The first question to ask yourself is whether the project manager needs assistance. If the project manager is one of your top people then you can ask them what help they need and take your lead from them. Otherwise, you may need to take a lead in deciding the strategy for sorting out the problem.

An important role you may have to play is to ensure that appropriately vigorous measures have been taken. As I have mentioned before, it is easy to underestimate how hard and fast you may need to react to a problem.

You may also need to take a high-profile role in handling the customers who are affected by the problem – often you will find that the team involved are more focused on solving the problem than they are on addressing the effects that the problem has on your customers.

Scenario 13

One of your key staff is rubbing other team members up the wrong way

The obvious solution here is the best – you need to explain to both sides how the other side perceives them. Another useful technique is to be visibly annoyed with both sides – statements such as 'I don't care who's right and who's wrong. I don't expect everyone to be friends but I do expect you all to act like professionals' can help to defuse emotion.

It is worth remembering that some level of tension within a team is quite normal, and seldom will it be possible to remove all such tensions – you have to manage them.

Scenario 14

You are told by your management to brief your staff with information that you think is probably untrue

I wanted to include this scenario for two reasons. First, because I do not know what the answer is. Second, because I suspect that there is no right answer. In fact, I suspect there is no good answer.

I moved from being a research scientist to being a manager. One of the things that struck me was that it was much easier to know if I was doing a good job as a research scientist than it was as a manager. As a researcher, I could usually measure in some way how good my work was. The same is not true of management. The world of the manager is often not black and white, it is various shades of grey. In this particular scenario, there are various shades of dark grey. If you toe the party line then you threaten your reputation for honesty. If you admit your doubts then your organisation will correctly accuse you of a lack of loyalty. Heads they win, tails you lose.

OK, so what would I do in this situation? I would give the briefing as provided to me, and I would say that I suspect there is more to this than meets the eye, but we will only find out the full picture in time.

Scenario 15

You have a project manager in your team who has a very laid-back approach to project management and does not seem to worry as much as you would about delivering projects on time and on budget. They have run a number of projects which, despite your worries, have come in on budget and on time. Do you deploy this person on a very important, high-visibility project and, if so, do you institute any additional controls?

I have encountered this situation on a number of occasions. In a previous chapter I said that when you delegate a task, you also delegate the ability to do that task differently from the way you would do it yourself. When I said this I had in mind the fact that the plan chosen to achieve the objective might well be substantially different from the plan you would have created. I think the principle extends to other areas that delegated authority is exercised in a different way from your own. I also think that people have a right to be judged by their results, and if this project manager has a record of delivering then they are entitled to your trust. Having said that, I have found it impossible not to be very diligent in reviewing progress with such people to ensure that I do not lose sleep on their behalf.

Scenario 16

You go to get yourself a coffee and find a group of your team joking about an incident that seriously breaks the health and safety rules

As a general rule I think that managers should not lose their tempers. I also think that you should only criticise staff in private. But there are times when the general rules do not apply. Personally, I think I would do a passable impression of a Titan rocket lifting off the pad. Flaming everyone liberally over such a gross breach of proper behaviour would be entirely appropriate and would show that you do not tolerate your team acting in such a way.

A related scenario ...

Scenario 17

You come across a situation where it is pretty clear that one member of your team is bullying another member of your team

I would be tempted to publicly tear a strip off the bully, but I think it would be better to give the bully a piece of my mind in private. I would not be at all worried if it was pretty obvious from my body language that I was furious as I marched the bully off for the dressing down. Because the issue reflects so badly on the bully, I think it would be better done in private.

If the scenario was changed to one where I overheard a racist joke, I think on balance it would be better to tear the strip off in public. Telling a racist joke shows an appalling lapse of judgement, but many of the people who might overhear your fury would think, 'There, but for the grace of God, go I'. As a result the humiliation the person suffered from the public telling off would be of a temporary nature. In the bullying situation, you might undermine the person for some considerable time to come.

Scenario 18

Your boss asks you to do something that you think is in your boss's best interests but will harm your organisation

There is no simple answer to this question, so I will try to dissect the possible responses you might make and analyse the reasons why you might choose the various responses.

There seem to me to be four possible courses of action, with varying degrees of forcefulness.

1 You do it without protest.

2 You tell your boss you are uncomfortable with the request and try to engage your boss in a discussion that you hope will lead to the request being withdrawn.

3 You refuse the request, saying politely why you feel it would be inappropriate.

4 You ask your boss's boss, or someone else in authority, what you should do.

How do you choose your response? Unfortunately this is one of those situations that is unlikely to be black or white – it will most likely be an infuriating shade of grey.

One key factor is the seriousness of the damage you might do to your organisation if you carry out your boss's orders. If the damage would be pretty minor then a less extreme action can be justified; but if the damage would be major, or the request is immoral or illegal, then No. 4 is your only acceptable response. Another good question to ask yourself is 'If my boss's boss finds out, how angry would they be that I had not reported the situation to them?'

The second major factor would be the personality of your boss. If they are an autocratic person likely to bear a grudge then you may be better off going for either a very weak (No. 1) or a very strong (No. 4) response. If they are usually fairly reasonable then a No. 2 response might well be appropriate. If they are fairly weak and cowardly then a No. 2 or No. 3 could work.

I am sorry I cannot offer more definite advice, but one reason for including this scenario was to show that there will be times when you will find yourself in 'no-win' situations where you have to make a choice from a number of seemingly unattractive options.

Scenario 19

This is a follow-on from Scenario 18. You decide what you are being asked to do is so serious that you tell your boss's boss, who doesn't want to know and says you must make your own decision

I made this a separate scenario because I feel that an important principle is involved. It is my view that if you raise a problem formally with your organisation, and that does not work, then you have discharged your responsibilities to the organisation. Further escalation can quickly get you a reputation as a trouble-maker and can easily damage your career.

Having had no satisfactory resolution of the problem from your boss's boss, I would either carry out the instructions of the boss or refuse. If the issue is solely one of damage to the organisation, I would probably just do it. If I were being asked to do something immoral or illegal I would refuse to do it and say politely why. Were the boss to continue to insist then I would ask that the instruction be put in writing – that will usually shut the boss up. If the boss puts it in writing, I would put my refusal in writing and send it to my boss with a copy to the boss's boss. At such times it is very useful to be a member of a trades union and I would certainly contact my TU representative for advice. This would make life very difficult in future dealings with your boss, but there are times when principles must be lived up to, and this is one of them.

Scenario 20

You have a new boss who turns out to be a micro-manager who keeps getting involved in unnecessarily detailed issues

I really wish I could tell you that telling your boss to butt out was the answer. This approach is high risk, and even if your boss takes the message without shooting you they are unlikely to mend their ways. It is possible in time that you will develop a relationship with your boss that will allow you to discuss his tendency to micro-manage. Failing that, or until your relationship has developed, you have to deal with the situation.

You have to realise, and if necessary get your team to realise, that there is very little you can do about it, and try to avoid getting stressed out by something you cannot change.

There are, however, a couple of things you can do to mitigate the damage ...

First, you should ensure that all the financial aspects of the team and all issues that impact on the bottom line are kept in perfect order. This is one of the best ways to reassure a micro-manager, and provides protection if they start to criticise you – someone who is delivering against their budget seldom gets shot.

Second, make sure you give the boss a monthly written progress report. This will provide both reassurance, by giving the boss extra visibility, and the protection of being able to show that you had highlighted areas of risk in good time.

A related scenario ...

> ### ☀ brilliant tip
>
> Know when to put things in writing. If you think that an issue may blow up at a later date, make sure you leave a paper or email trail that you can refer back to in the future. It is also worth keeping a log book in which you can note details down in chronological order. My log book has got me out of trouble so many times that I never begrudge the effort of filling it in daily.

Scenario 21

You have a new boss who blames you, rather than backs you up, when things go wrong

My advice is virtually identical to that given for the last scenario, with one addition.

Be very conservative in your budgeting, because your boss is not going to back you up if you fail to make an ambitious target. Also be sure not to overdeliver or your boss will inflate your next year's targets. It is fairly easy to push revenue from one year into the next, to bring yourself in closer to budget, and you can then offer a higher budget target yourself next year, knowing that you are already part way to meeting it.

You may want to adopt a similarly conservative approach to deadlines and targets that come up during the year.

Conclusions

You cannot learn management from a book, but you can gain a better understanding of why some things work and why other things can be almost guaranteed to fail. You don't have to implement everything immediately – just try out some new ideas and see if they work for you.

I have only scratched the surface in a number of areas, such as marketing and business strategy, and hope you feel motivated to continue reading other books about these topics.

The job of a manager and leader is pretty daunting. This book tries to show how critically important the lower levels of management in an organisation are to the financial health of the organisation and the well-being of its staff. One of my purposes in writing this book was to give managers greater pride in their jobs. After all, brilliant management is easy to understand but very hard to do.

Good luck!

Index

the brilliant series

Fast and engaging, the *Brilliant* series works hard to make sure you stand out from the crowd. Each *Brilliant* book has been carefully crafted to ensure everything you read is practical and applicable – to help you make a difference now.

brilliant Project Management
What the best project managers know, do and say
9780273722328

brilliant Leader
What the best leaders know, do and say
9780273720591

brilliant Coaching
How to be a brilliant coach in your workplace
9780273717355

brilliant Networking
What the best networkers know, do and say
9780273743217

brilliant Selling
What the best salespeople know, do and say
9780273726463

brilliant Pitch
What to know, do and say to make the perfect pitch.
9780273725114

brilliant Marketing
What the best marketers know, do and say
9780273721239

brilliant Negotiations
What the best negotiators know, do and say
9780273712350

brilliant Decision Making
Take control of your career, relationships, health and happiness
9780273734147

brilliant IDEA
9780273714804

brilliant Presentation
What the best presenters know, do and say
9780273730675

brilliant Budgets and Forecasts
Your practical guide to preparing and presenting financial information
9780273730910

9780273720799

9780273727347

9780273721826

9780273738077

9780273737452

9780273742555

9780273744092

9780273724902

9780273732556

9780273740544

9780273735885

9780273723271

Whatever your level, we'll get you to the next one. It's all about you. Get ready to shine!

Prentice Hall
is an imprint of